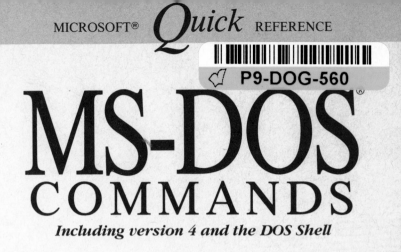

P9-DOG-560

MS-DOS®
COMMANDS
Including version 4 and the DOS Shell

VAN WOLVERTON

Microsoft
P R E S S
®

PUBLISHED BY
Microsoft Press
A Division of Microsoft Corporation
One Microsoft Way
Redmond, Washington 98052-6399

Library of Congress Cataloging-in-Publication Data
Wolverton, Van, 1939-
    MS-DOS commands : Microsoft quick reference / Van Wolverton.
        p.   cm.
    ISBN 1-55615-289-2
    1. MS-DOS (Computer operating system)   I. Title.
QA76.76.063W63   1990
005.4'46--dc20   89-14285
                                                                         CIP

Printed and bound in the United States of America.

1 2 3 4 5 6 7 8 9   RARA   4 3 2 1 0

Distributed to the book trade in Canada by General Publishing Company, Ltd.

Distributed to the book trade outside the United States and Canada by Penguin
Books Ltd.

Penguin Books Ltd., Harmondsworth, Middlesex, England
Penguin Books Australia Ltd., Ringwood, Victoria, Australia
Penguin Books N.Z. Ltd., 182–190 Wairau Road, Auckland 10, New Zealand

British Cataloging in Publication Data available

As used in this quick reference, DOS refers to the Microsoft MS-DOS
operating system and the IBM version of the MS-DOS operating system,
also known as PC-DOS.

Project Editor: Nancy Siadek   **Technical Editor:** Dail Magee, Jr.

Contents

Introduction

This quick reference guide covers the commands and editing keys for DOS versions 2.0 through 4. DOS, batch, configuration, Edlin, and Shell commands are presented in alphabetic order within each group. Each entry includes the full form of the command, a brief description of the command and its parameters, and usually an example of its use.

Some commands have many possible forms. When you must enter parameters exactly, they are shown precisely as you must type them. When a parameter is shown in *italic*, it represents a variable that you must supply, such as the name of a file, disk drive, or output device. Items in brackets are optional, and you include them only under specific circumstances. The ¦ symbol means that you should choose only one of the options within the brackets. DO NOT TYPE THE BRACKETS OR THE ¦ SYMBOL.

The parameters for DOS commands that you will encounter in this quick reference guide include the following:

drive: A letter referring to a disk drive, followed by a required colon.

filename   The name of a file, usually followed by an extension. For example:

`report.jan`

path   One or more directory entries, each separated from the previous one by a backslash (\). For example:

`\mkt\reports`

pathname   One or more directory names followed by a filename, each name separated from the previous one by a backslash (\). For example:

`\mkt\reports\report.jan`

switches   Controls for commands, each beginning with a slash (/). For example:

`/p`

DOS Commands

The system prompt (such as A> or C>) tells you that DOS is at the command level, ready to accept commands. The letter in the system prompt identifies the current drive; you can change the current drive by typing the new drive letter, followed by a colon, and pressing the Enter key.

If you make an error typing a command, you can press the Backspace key to erase the last letter typed. When you have typed the command correctly, execute it by pressing the Enter key.

Append

Syntax:

append [/x][/e]

or

append [*drive:*][*path*][;[*drive:*][*path*] . . .]

or

append ;

or

append [*path*] [/x[:on]] [/path:on]

or

append [*path*] [/x:off] [/path:off]

Description:

Tells DOS to look for data files in the specified drive and directory.

/x or /x:on extends the Append data path, making it available to programs that use the Exec (INT 21H, Function 4BH), Search First (INT 21H, Function 11H), or Find First (INT 21H, Function 4EH) function. If you do not specify /x or /x:on, programs can access the data path only if they use the Open File (INT 21H, Function 0FH), Open Handle (INT 21H, Function 3DH), or Get File Size (INT 21H, Function 23H) function. If you specify /x or /x:on, you cannot specify *drive:path*; you must enter another Append command to define the data path. You can use the /x switch only the first time you enter an Append command after starting DOS. The /x:on switch is available only in version 4; you use this switch to activate a previously defined data path that you disabled with another Append command that included an /x:off switch.

/e makes the Append data path part of the DOS environment. You can use /e only the first time you enter an Append command after starting DOS. If you specify /e, you cannot specify *drive:path*; you must enter another Append command to define the data path.

The /x and /e switches are available only in versions 3.3 and later. The /path:on and /path:off switches are available only in version 4.

drive: is the drive to be searched. If you omit *drive:*, DOS assumes the current drive.

path is the name of the directory or subdirectory to be searched. You can enter more than one *drive:path* by separating them with semicolons.

/path:on tells the Append command to search for data files that have a drive letter, a path, or both as a part of their name.

/path:off tells the Append command to ignore data files that have a drive letter, a path, or both as a part of their name.

An Append command followed only by a semicolon removes any search paths previously set with Append.

An Append command with no parameters displays the current search path for data files.

Warning: When an assigned drive is to be part of the search path, you must use the Append command before the Assign command.

Example:

To set the search path for data files to include the \LETTERS and \REPORTS directories in drive B and the \MEMOS directory in drive A, type:

```
append b:\letters;b:\reports;a:\memos
```

Assign

Syntax:

assign [*drive1* [=] *drive2* [. . .]]

Description:

Refers requests for one disk drive to another disk drive.

drive1 is the drive you don't want to use (the letter to be assigned to a different drive).

drive2 is the drive that is to be used in place of *drive1*.

Do not type a colon after any drive letter.

Multiple drive assignments can be made with a single Assign command.

If you type Assign alone, DOS cancels any assignments currently in effect.

This command is available in PC-DOS versions 2.0 and later and in MS-DOS versions 3.0 and later.

Warning: Because Assign affects *all* requests for a drive, you should use it with caution, especially if the reassignment involves a hard disk. Always bear in mind that some DOS commands, such as Erase, delete existing files from the disk in the specified drive. The Assign command also hides drive characteristics from programs that require detailed knowledge of the drive size and format, such as

Backup, Restore, Label, Join, Substitute, or Print. The Format, Diskcopy, Diskcomp, and System commands ignore any drive reassignments made with Assign.

Example:

Suppose you have a graphics program that requires all data files to be in drive B, but you want to use your hard disk (drive C) for data files. To tell DOS to assign all requests for drive B to drive C instead, type:

```
assign b=c
```

Attribute

Syntax:

attrib [+r¦−r] [+a¦−a] [*drive:*]*pathname* [/s]

Description:

Lets you protect files by making them read-only (unable to be changed or erased); and, in versions 3.2 and later, allows you to set or remove a file's archive flag for use with the Backup or Xcopy command.

+r tells DOS to make the file read-only.

−r tells DOS to let the file be changed or erased.

+a tells DOS to set the file's archive flag.

−a tells DOS to remove the file's archive flag.

drive:pathname is the name and location of the file whose read-only or archive flag status is to be displayed or changed. Wildcard characters are permitted.

/s tells Attribute to process all subdirectories in *pathname*. (Available only in versions 3.3 and later.)

If you enter the Attrib command with only a pathname, Attrib displays the name of the file, preceded by an *R* if the file is read-only and, in versions 3.2 and later, preceded by an *A* if the file's archive bit is set.

This command is available only in versions 3.0 and later.

Examples:

To make BANK.TXT (in the current drive and directory) a
read-only file, type:

```
attrib +r bank.txt
```

To remove the read-only protection, type:

```
attrib -r bank.txt
```

To set the archive flag on all files in the directory
\SYSTEM on drive C, including all files stored in subdirectories of \SYSTEM, type:

```
attrib +a c:\system\*.* /s
```

Backup

Syntax:

backup [*drive1:*]*pathname drive2:* [/s][/m][/a][/p][/f:*size*]
[/d:*date*][/t:*time*][/L:[*drive:*][*path*]*filename*]

Description:

Makes backup copies of files from one disk to another;
erases files already on the target disk, unless you include
the /a switch. If you back up files to a hard disk, creates a
\BACKUP directory in which to store the files.

drive1:pathname is the name and location of the files to be
backed up. Wildcard characters are permitted. If you do not
specify a drive, Backup assumes the current drive. If you
do not specify a path, Backup assumes the current directory. If you do not specify a filename, Backup backs up all
files in that directory.

drive2: specifies the destination disk to receive the backup
files. This parameter is not optional.

/s backs up the contents of all subdirectories.

/m backs up only those files modified since the last backup.

/a adds the file(s) to the existing files on the destination
disk (does not erase the destination disk). Version 4 of the

Backup command does not accept this switch if the existing files were backed up using version 3.2 or earlier of
Backup.

/p packs the destination disk with as many files as possible,
even if a subdirectory must be created to hold some of the
files. (Available only in MS-DOS versions 2.0 through 3.1.)

/f:*size* formats the target disk if it isn't already formatted.
For this switch to work, the Format command must be ac-
cessible via the current command path. In MS-DOS version
3.3, the /f switch has no size parameter, and the disk in the
destination drive is formatted to match the capacity of that
drive. In MS-DOS version 4, *size* is one of the following
values:

Disk size	*size* values
160-KB single-sided, 5¼-inch	160, 160K, 160KB
180-KB single-sided, 5¼-inch	180, 180K, 180KB
320-KB double-sided, 5¼-inch	320, 320K, 320KB
360-KB double-sided, 5¼-inch	360, 360K, 360KB
720-KB double-sided, 3½-inch	720, 720K, 720KB
1.2-MB double-sided, 5¼-inch	1200, 1200K, 1200KB, 1.2, 1.2M, 1.2MB
1.44-MB double-sided, 3½-inch	1440, 1440M, 1440MB, 1.4, 1.4M, 1.44MB

/d:*date* backs up only those files modified on or after *date*.
The date format depends on whether the Country command
is in effect; the default is *mm-dd-yy*.

/t:*time* backs up only those files modified at or after *time*.
The time format depends on whether the Country command
is in effect; the default is *hh:mm:ss*. (Not supported in all
implementations of Backup.)

/L:*filename* creates a log file of the files that were backed
up. In versions 3.2 and earlier, only the *filename* option is
permitted; for these versions the log file is placed in the
root directory of the source disk. In version 4, the *drive:path*
option allows you to specify the location of the log file. If
you omit either option, the current drive and/or path is
assumed. If you do not specify a filename, Backup creates
a file named BACKUP.LOG and places the log entries there.

PC-DOS versions 3.0 and later and MS-DOS versions 3.1 and later support all combinations of media.

Warning: You should not use Backup with a drive affected by a Join command; if you do, you might not be able to restore the files with the Restore command. You should also not use Backup with a drive affected by an Append, Assign, or Substitute command.

Note: You cannot use version 3.2 or earlier of the Restore command to restore files backed up with version 4 of the Backup command.

Example:

To back up all the files in \MKT\BUDGET from the current drive to drive B, type:

```
backup \mkt\budget b:
```

Backup then prompts you to check that the correct disk is in the drive. Backup also prompts you to insert additional disks if the disk in drive B becomes full.

Break

Syntax:

break [on ¦ off]

Description:

Tells the operating system how often it should check for a Ctrl-C, the key sequence you use to terminate a program or a batch file.

By default, DOS checks for Ctrl-C when reading from or writing to a character device, such as a printer, screen, or auxiliary port. The Break On command instructs DOS also to check for Ctrl-C each time a system call occurs.

If you type *break* alone, Break displays a message informing you whether Break is on or off.

Examples:

To have DOS also check for a Ctrl-C whenever a system call is made, type:

```
break on
```

To restore the default condition, type:

```
break off
```

Change Code Page

Syntax:

chcp [*nnn*]

Description:

Changes or displays the number of the code page that DOS uses for all devices that support code-page switching.

nnn is the number of the new code page:

Code-page number	Code page
437	American (English)
850	Multilingual
860	Portuguese
863	French-Canadian
865	Nordic

If you omit *nnn*, Chcp displays the current (active) page. The current code page is the character set DOS uses to display characters. Chcp displays an error message if the specified code page isn't compatible with a device or if the specified code page wasn't prepared with the *codepage prepare* parameter of the Mode command.

Note: You must execute the National Language Support Function (Nlsfunc) before you can use the Change Code Page command.

The Chcp command is available only in versions 3.3 and later.

Examples:

To change the current code page to Nordic (assuming it has already been prepared), type:

```
chcp 865
```

To display the current code page, type:

```
chcp
```

Assuming the first example was successful, Chcp displays:

```
Active code page: 865
```

Change Directory

Syntax:

chdir [*drive:*][*path*]

Description:

Displays the name of or changes the current directory. (Can be abbreviated as cd.)

drive: can be used to change the current directory in another drive to *path*. This parameter does not cause the system to change drives, and the directory from which you entered the command will remain the current directory. If you enter *drive:* without *path*, the current directory in *drive:* is displayed.

path is the name of the directory that is to become the current directory. If *path* includes one or more subdirectories, you must precede each one with a backslash.

If you enter Chdir without parameters, it displays the current directory of the current drive.

Examples:

To change the current directory to the directory named \DATA, type:

```
cd \data
```

To change to the \LETTERS subdirectory of the \WORD directory, type:

```
cd \word\letters
```

To back up one directory level closer to the root directory, type:

```
cd ..
```

To change to the root directory, type:

```
cd \
```

Check Disk

Syntax:

chkdsk [*drive:*][*pathname*] [/v][/f]

Description:

Analyzes the allocation of storage on a disk and displays the disk's volume name and creation date, a summary report of the space occupied by files and directories, the number of bytes in bad sectors, the number of bytes free, and the total system memory. In version 4, Chkdsk also shows the disk's serial number, the size in bytes of each allocation unit, the total number of allocation units, and the number of available allocation units. In all versions, Chkdsk displays a message informing you whether or not noncontiguous files were found.

drive:pathname is the name and location of the file to be checked. Wildcard characters are permitted. If you omit *drive:*, Chkdsk assumes the current drive. If you omit *pathname*, Chkdsk checks the entire disk.

/v displays the name of each directory and file on the disk as it checks.

/f tells Chkdsk to correct any errors it finds, after prompting for permission. If you do not include the /f switch, Chkdsk does not convert lost chains into clusters, even if you respond *y* to the prompt.

Note: You cannot use Chkdsk with a drive affected by an Assign, a Join, or a Substitute command or with a drive assigned to a network.

Example:

To check all files on the disk in drive B and display the directory names and filenames, type:

```
chkdsk b:*.* /v
```

Clear Screen

Syntax:

cls

Description:

Clears the screen and displays the system prompt.

Example:

To erase everything on the screen and display the system prompt in the upper left corner, type:

```
cls
```

Command Processor

Syntax:

command [*drive:*][*path*] [*cttydev*][/e:*nnnnn*][/p][/c *string*]

Description:

Allows you to invoke a copy of the parent command processor and, optionally, change some of its characteristics. (The command processor is the part of DOS that issues prompts, interprets commands and batch files, and loads and executes application programs.)

drive:path specifies the drive and/or the directory to be searched for COMMAND.COM when its transient portion needs to be reloaded.

cttydev specifies a character device to be used for input and output instead of the default keyboard and monitor. (Not available in PC-DOS.)

/e:*nnnnn* specifies the initial size, in bytes, of the command processor's environment block (versions 3.2 and later). The maximum size is 32768 bytes; the default is 160 bytes. The number is rounded up to the next paragraph boundary (evenly divisible by 16) if appropriate.

/p disables the Exit command and causes the newly loaded command processor to be fixed permanently in memory.

/c *string* causes the secondary command processor to behave as a transient program. It executes the command or program specified by *string* and then exits and returns control to the parent processor. If you do not include /c *string* in the command line, then the secondary copy of COMMAND.COM remains in memory until an Exit command is executed. When used in combination with other switches, this must be the last switch on the command line.

Examples:

To execute the batch file MENU2.BAT from the batch file MENU1.BAT and then resume execution of MENU1.BAT, include the following line in MENU1.BAT:

```
command /c menu2
```

Note: The technique in this example is unnecessary in versions 3.3 and later, which include the Call batch command.

To load a secondary command processor permanently into memory and transfer the input and output device to a terminal attached to a serial port, type:

```
command aux /p
```

Compare

Syntax:

comp [*drive:*][*pathname1*] [*drive:*][*pathname2*]

Description:

Compares two files or sets of files to see whether their contents are the same. This command is available in all versions of PC-DOS and in MS-DOS versions 3.3 and later.

drive:pathname1 and *drive:pathname2* are the names and locations of the files to be compared. Wildcard characters are permitted. If you include no drive or path, Compare assumes the current directory of the current drive. If you omit either filename, Compare prompts you for the missing information.

Example:

To compare REPORT.TXT in drive B with BUDGET.FEB in drive A, type:

```
comp b:report.txt a:budget.feb
```

Copy: Combine Files

Syntax:

copy [*drive:*][*path*]*source*[+[[*drive:*][*path*]*source*] . . .]
    [*drive:*][*path*]*target* [/a][/b][/v]

Description:

Combines two or more source files into the specified target file, creating *target* if it doesn't already exist, or combines one or more source files into the first source file specified in the command line.

drive:path source is the name and location of the files to be combined. Wildcard characters are permitted. You can also specify a list of several filenames separated by plus signs.

Caution: If any file in a list separated by plus signs doesn't exist, Copy goes on to the next name without telling you that the file doesn't exist.

drive:path target is the name and location of the file that results from combining the source files. If you specify *target*, Copy combines the source files into *target*. If you omit *target*, Copy combines the source files into the first source file.

/a indicates that the file is an ASCII (text-only) file. Applied to *source* files, /a copies data up to, but not including, the first Ctrl-Z character encountered in each file. Applied to *target*, /a appends a Ctrl-Z character to the *target* file as the last character in the file.

/b indicates that the file is a binary file.

/v performs read-after-write verification of the destination file(s).

Note: The /a and /b switches affect the filename immediately preceding them and all subsequent filenames in the command line, until another /a or /b switch is encountered.

Warning: When Copy concatenates to the first source file in a series, the original (unconcatenated) version of that file is lost.

Examples:

To combine BANK.DOC and REPORT.DOC into a new file named BANKRPT.DOC (while keeping the original files intact), type:

```
copy bank.doc+report.doc bankrpt.doc
```

To concatenate BUDGET.FEB and BUDGET.MAR into the existing source file BUDGET.JAN, type:

```
copy budget.jan+budget.feb+budget.mar
```

Copy: Copy from a Device

Syntax:

copy *source target*

Description:

Copies the output of a device to a file or another device.

source is the name of the device whose output is to be copied.

target is the name of the file or device to which the output is to be copied. If *target* is a filename, it can include a path but no wildcards.

Warning: Be sure that both the source and target devices exist; if you try to copy to or from a device that doesn't exist or isn't ready, DOS might stop running, forcing you to restart the system.

Examples:

To copy from the keyboard (CON) to the printer (PRN), be sure the printer is turned on, and then type:

```
copy con prn
```

To copy from the keyboard (CON) to a file named MYFILE.TXT, type:

```
copy con myfile.txt
```

In both examples, when you have finished typing the file, you must press F6 or Ctrl-Z and then Enter to terminate the Copy command.

Copy: Copy a File to a Device

Syntax:

copy [*drive:*]*pathname device* [/a][/b]

Description:

Copies a file to a device.

drive:pathname is the name and location of the file to be sent to a device. Wildcard characters are permitted.

device is the name of the device to which *pathname* is to be sent.

/a indicates that the file is an ASCII (text-only) file. When used, /a copies data from *pathname* up to, but not including, the first Ctrl-Z character encountered in the file.

/b indicates that the file is a binary file.

You cannot use the Copy command to send output to COM or AUX serial ports.

Warning: Be sure *device* exists; if you try to send a file to a device that doesn't exist or isn't ready, DOS might stop running, forcing you to restart the system.

Examples:

To send a copy of each file with the extension .TXT in the current drive and directory to the printer, type:

```
copy *.txt prn
```

To send a copy of the file REPORT.TXT to the screen, type:

```
copy report.txt con
```

Copy: Copy a File to a File

Syntax:

copy [*drive:*]*pathname1* [*drive:*][*pathname2*] [/a][/b][/v]

Description:

Copies a file to another file.

drive:pathname1 is the name and location of the source file.

drive:pathname2 is the name and location of the target file.

Wildcard characters are permitted in both filenames.

If you specify a drive other than the current drive for *pathname1* and omit *drive:pathname2*, *pathname1* is copied to the current directory of the current drive. If you specify only a drive letter for *pathname2*, *pathname1* is copied to the disk in the drive you specify and given the same filename.

If *pathname1* doesn't exist, Copy displays the pathname you specified, followed by *File not found* and *0 File(s) copied*, and returns to command level. If *pathname2* doesn't exist, Copy creates it. If *pathname2* already exists, Copy replaces its contents with those of *pathname1*.

Warning: This latter situation is the same as erasing the existing file, so be careful not to give the copy of a file the same name as an existing file that you want to keep.

/a indicates that the file is an ASCII (text-only) file. When applied to *pathname1*, /a copies data up to, but not including, the first Ctrl-Z character encountered. When applied to *pathname2*, /a appends a Ctrl-Z character to the file as the last character of the new file.

/b indicates that the file is a binary file.

/v performs read-after-write verification of the destination file(s).

Note: The /a and /b switches affect the filename immediately preceding them and all subsequent filenames in the command line, until another /a or /b switch is encountered.

Examples:

To make a copy of the file REPORT.DOC on the same disk and name the copy RESULTS.DOC, type:

```
copy report.doc results.doc
```

To copy the file REPORT.DOC from drive A to the current drive, giving the file the same name, type:

```
copy a:report.doc
```

To copy the file REPORT.DOC from the current drive to the disk in drive A, giving the file the same name, type:

```
copy report.doc a:
```

Ctty   (Change I/O Device)

Syntax:

ctty *device*

Description:

Specifies the character device to be used as the standard input and standard output device.

device is a logical character device name (AUX, COM1, COM2, or CON).

DOS ordinarily uses the computer's built-in keyboard and screen as the standard input and standard output device. Ctty allows you to assign instead another character device as the standard device.

Examples:

To redirect keyboard input and screen output to a terminal attached to a serial port (AUX), type:

```
ctty aux
```

To restore control to the console (CON, the computer's built-in keyboard and screen), type:

```
ctty con
```

Date

Syntax:

date [*month-day-year*]

Description:

Sets the system date.

month is a number from 1 through 12.

day is a number from 1 through 31.

year is a number from 80 through 99 (for 1980 through 1999).
If you use four digits to enter the year, you can enter dates
through 12-31-2079.

If you don't include any parameters, Date displays the current setting of the system date and prompts you to enter a
new date.

Note: In MS-DOS versions 2.1 and later and in PC-DOS versions 3.0 and later, if a Country command was used in the
CONFIG.SYS file when the system was started or, in MS-
DOS versions 3.3 and later and PC-DOS versions 3.0
and later, if the Select command was used to configure a
country-specific system disk, the format for the date might
be different.

Example:

To set the system date to January 1, 1989, type:

```
date 1-1-89
```

Delete

Syntax:

del [*drive:*]*pathname* [/p]

Description:

Deletes a file or group of files.

drive:pathname is the name and location of the file or group
of files to be deleted. Wildcard characters are permitted. If
you omit *drive:*, Del assumes the current drive.

/p causes Del to prompt you before deleting each file.

You cannot use Del to delete a directory. (See Remove
Directory.)

Warning: The action of the Del command is final, so be
sure you have typed the correct drive letter, filename, and
extension before you press Enter.

Example:

To delete all files in the \OLD directory in drive B with a
.TXT extension, type:

```
del b:\old\*.txt
```

Directory

Syntax:

dir [*drive:*][*path*][*filename*] [/w][/p]

Description:

Displays a directory listing of files on a disk, the number of
files in the specified directory, and the number of bytes
available on the disk.

drive: is the drive in which the directory to be listed is located. If you specify only *drive:*, Dir displays all files in
the current directory of that drive.

path is the name of the directory whose files are to be
displayed.

filename is the name of a specific file to be listed. Only the
entry for that file is displayed. Wildcard characters are
permitted.

If you enter Dir with no parameters, the entries for all files
in the current directory of the current drive are displayed.

/w displays filenames and extensions only, in five columns
across the screen.

/p displays the entries one screenful at a time.

Examples:

To display the current directory of drive C in the wide format, type:

```
dir c: /w
```

To display the directory of \LETTERS in drive B one
screenful at a time, type:

```
dir b:\letters /p
```

Disk Compare

Syntax:

diskcomp [*drive1:* [*drive2:*]] [/1][/8]

Description:

Compares two entire floppy disks. (For comparing sets of files, see Compare or File Compare.)

drive1: and *drive2:* are the drives containing the floppy disks to be compared. If you omit *drive2:*, Diskcomp compares the floppy disk in *drive1:* with the floppy disk in the current drive. If you omit both drives, Diskcomp assumes you want to use only the current drive and prompts you to switch floppy disks during the comparison.

/1 compares only the first sides of floppy disks, even if the disks and drives are double-sided.

/8 limits the comparison to the first 8 sectors per track, even if the floppy disk in *drive1:* has 9 or 15 sectors per track.

This command is available in PC-DOS versions 2.0 and later and in MS-DOS versions 3.2 and later.

Note: You cannot use Diskcomp to compare disks of different types (such as a 360-KB disk with a 1.2-MB disk). In addition, you cannot use Diskcomp with a hard disk, with a drive affected by a Substitute command, or with a drive assigned to a network. You should not use Diskcomp with a drive affected by a Join command. Diskcomp ignores drive assignments made with an Assign command.

Examples:

With a two-floppy-disk-drive system, to compare the disk in drive A with the disk in drive B, type:

```
diskcomp a: b:
```

With a single-disk-drive system, type:

```
diskcomp
```

and follow the prompts.

To compare the disk in drive B with the disk in the current drive, type:

```
diskcomp b:
```

Disk Copy

Syntax:

diskcopy [*drive1:*] [*drive2:*] [/1]

Description:

Makes a duplicate of a floppy disk.

drive1: is the drive that contains the floppy disk to be copied.

drive2: is the drive that contains the floppy disk that is to receive the copy. If you omit *drive2:*, Diskcopy copies the disk in *drive1:* to the floppy disk in the current drive.

/1 copies only the first side of a floppy disk. (Available only in PC-DOS and in MS-DOS versions 3.2 and later.)

PC-DOS versions of Diskcopy format the disk in *drive2:* before copying; MS-DOS versions of Diskcopy prior to 3.2 require that you first format the target disk.

If needed, PC-DOS versions give the floppy disk in *drive2:* the same number of sides and sectors per track as the floppy disk in *drive1:*. If the floppy disk in *drive1:* has 9 sectors per track and the floppy disk in *drive2:* was already formatted with 8 sectors per track, Diskcopy reformats the floppy disk in *drive2:* to 9 sectors before copying.

You cannot use Diskcopy to copy to a disk of a different type (such as a 360-KB disk to a 1.2-MB disk).

Note: You cannot use Diskcopy with a drive affected by a Substitute command or with a drive assigned to a network. You should not use Diskcopy with a drive affected by a Join command. Diskcopy ignores drive reassignments made with an Assign command.

Examples:

With a two-floppy-disk-drive system, to copy the disk in drive A to the disk in drive B, type:

```
diskcopy a: b:
```

With a single-disk-drive system, type:

```
diskcopy
```

and follow the prompts.

Dosshell

Syntax:

dosshell

Description:

Starts the DOS Shell. (See "Shell Commands.")

Warning: Use the Exit command instead of the Dosshell command to return to the DOS Shell if you previously exited the Shell by pressing Shift-F9 or by selecting the Command Prompt item from the Main Group. Otherwise, extra copies of the DOS Shell are created, which reduces the amount of memory available to your programs.

Example:

To start the DOS Shell, type:

```
dosshell
```

Erase

Syntax:

erase [*drive:*]*pathname* [/p]

Description:

Erases one or more files.

drive:pathname is the name and location of the file or group of files to be erased. Wildcard characters are permitted. If you omit *drive:*, Erase assumes the current drive.

/p causes Erase to prompt you before erasing each file.

You cannot use Erase to erase a directory. (See Remove Directory.)

Warning: The action of the Erase command is final, so be sure you have typed the correct drive letter, filename, and extension before you press Enter.

Examples:

To erase the file named BUDGET.APR on the disk in the current drive, type:

```
erase budget.apr
```

To erase all files with an extension of .TXT on the floppy disk in drive B, type:

```
erase b:*.txt
```

Exe2bin   (Executable to Binary Conversion)

Syntax:

exe2bin [*drive:*]*pathname1* [*drive:*][*pathname2*]

Description:

Converts an executable file (a file with an .EXE extension) to a binary-image file (a file with a .BIN extension). If the executable file meets certain requirements, you can rename the resulting binary-image file as a command file (a file with a .COM extension); it will then run faster than its EXE counterpart. This is an advanced DOS command, and you should refer to the documentation that came with your operating system before you attempt to use it.

Exit

Syntax:

exit

Description:

Terminates a secondary copy of the command processor invoked by the Command command or by the DOS Shell. Control returns to the parent program or command processor from which the command processor was invoked.

Exit has no effect if the secondary command processor was loaded with the /p (permanent) switch or if it is the original command processor (the one loaded when the computer is turned on or restarted with Ctrl-Alt-Del).

Fastopen

Syntax:

fastopen [*drive:*[=*nnn*] [. . .]] [/x]

or

fastopen [*drive:*[=([*nnn*],*mmm*)][. . .]] [/x]

Description:

Reduces access time to frequently used files by maintaining a list of their names and locations. (Available only in versions 3.3 and later.)

drive: is the letter of the drive whose files and subdirectories you want DOS to remember. *drive:* must refer to a hard disk.

nnn is the number of files Fastopen will track; it must be in the range 10 through 999. The default for PC-DOS is 34; the default for MS-DOS is 10.

mmm is the number of file-extent entries Fastopen will track; it must be in the range 1 through 999. If you include *mmm*, you must enclose *nnn* (if specified), a comma, and *mmm* in parentheses. (Available only in version 4.)

/x allows Fastopen to use expanded memory. (Available only in version 4.)

You can specify a maximum of four hard disks in a single Fastopen command.

You can use the Fastopen command only once per session. If you want to change the Fastopen settings again, you must restart DOS. Note that Fastopen uses approximately 40 bytes of memory for the name and location of each file in the list.

Each time you open a file, Fastopen adds that file's name and location to the list. If the list is full, the name and location of the oldest accessed file is dropped from the list. Thus, if a particular file is accessed frequently, its name and location will probably remain on the list.

Note: You cannot use Fastopen with a drive affected by an Assign, a Join, or a Substitute command or with a drive assigned to a network.

Example:

To tell DOS to keep a list of the names and locations of the last 70 files accessed in drive C, type:

```
fastopen c:=70
```

File Compare

Syntax:

fc [/b][/a][/c][/L][/ Lb *n*][/n][/t][/w][/*nnnn*]
    [*drive:*]*pathname1* [*drive:*]*pathname2*

Description:

Compares two text files containing lines of ASCII text or two binary files containing data of any type. Lists on the video display the differences between the two files.

/b forces a byte-by-byte (binary) comparison; files do not have to be ASCII files. This is the default when the file extension is .EXE, .COM, .SYS, .OBJ, .LIB, or .BIN. You can use this switch only with /*nnnn*.

/a causes abbreviated output of the differences found in an ASCII file comparison.

/c causes case to be ignored when comparing alphabetic characters.

/L forces a line-by-line comparison of two ASCII text files. This is the default when the file extension is not .EXE, .COM, .SYS, .OBJ, .LIB, or .BIN.

/Lb *n* sets the size of the internal line buffer to *n* lines. (The default value is 100.)

/n includes line numbers in the output of an ASCII file comparison.

/t causes tabs in text files to be compared literally. (The default treats tabs as spaces with stops at each eighth character position.)

/w causes leading and trailing spaces and tabs in text-file lines to be ignored and consecutive spaces and tabs within a line to be compressed to a single space.

/*nnnn* is the number of lines that must match to resynchronize during an ASCII file comparison. (In versions 3.2 and later, the default value is 2, in versions earlier than 3.2, the range is 1 through 9 and the default value is 3.)

drive:pathname1 is the name and location of the first file to be compared.

drive:pathname2 is the name and location of the second file to be compared. Wildcard characters are not permitted in either filename.

This command is available only in MS-DOS. The /a, /L, /Lb *n*, /n, and /t switches are available only in versions 3.1 and later.

Examples:

To do a line-by-line comparison of the ASCII (text-only)
file MYFILE.TXT with the file YOURFILE.LTR, type:

```
fc myfile.txt yourfile.ltr
```

To force a byte-by-byte comparison of BUDGET.JAN with
FORECAST.JAN, type:

```
fc /b budget.jan forecast.jan
```

Find

Syntax:

find [/v][/c][/n] *"string"* [*drive:*][*pathname*]
  [[*drive:*][*pathname*] ...]

Description:

Searches input lines for a string of characters you specify.

/v displays all lines that do not contain *string*.

/c displays only the total number of lines found.

/n displays each line found, preceded by its line number in
the file. This switch is ignored if you use it with /c.

If you enter the Find command with none of these switches,
the command displays all lines that contain *string*.

string is the string of characters you want to search for. You
must enclose the string in quotation marks. The Find command distinguishes between uppercase and lowercase
letters.

drive:pathname is the name and location of the file to be
searched. If you omit *drive:pathname*, the Find command
searches the keyboard input. (You terminate keyboard input
by pressing Ctrl-Z or F6.) You can include several different
filenames in a single Find command simply by separating
them with spaces.

Example:

To display the lines containing *cons* in the file PHONE.TXT in the current drive and precede each line by a number indicating its position in the file, type:

```
find /n "cons" phone.txt
```

Fixed Disk

Syntax:

fdisk

Description:

Starts a menu-driven program that allows you to perform hard-disk-management tasks (such as creating a DOS partition on the hard disk) or to tell DOS which partition is the active partition (the partition DOS should use when initializing the system from the hard disk).

This command is available only in PC-DOS versions 2.0 and later and in MS-DOS versions 3.2 and later.

Note: You cannot use Fdisk with a drive affected by a Join or a Substitute command or with a drive assigned to a network.

Example:

To start the Fdisk program, type:

```
fdisk
```

Format

Syntax:

format [*drive:*] [/1][/4][/8][/o][/v[:*label*]][/b][/n:*xx*][/t:*yy*]
    [/f:*size*][/s]

Description:

Prepares a disk so that DOS can store files on it and erases any existing data on the disk. You can make a system disk (a disk capable of booting the system) by using the /s switch.

drive: is the drive that contains the floppy disk to be formatted. If you omit *drive:*, Format formats the floppy disk in the current drive.

/1 formats only one side of a floppy disk. (Not available in MS-DOS versions 2.0 through 3.1.)

/4 formats a double-sided disk in a high-capacity drive. (Available in PC-DOS versions 3.0 and later and in MS-DOS versions 3.2 and later.)

/8 formats a floppy disk with eight sectors per track. (Not available in MS-DOS versions 2.0 through 3.1.)

/o formats a disk that is compatible with PC-DOS versions 1.x. (Available only in MS-DOS versions 2.0 through 3.1.)

/v tells Format that you want to give the floppy disk a volume label; Format prompts you for the label. To bypass the prompt, you can type a colon and the label immediately following the switch.

/b formats a disk with eight sectors per track and allocates space for DOS. DOS is not written to the disk. (See System.) This switch cannot be used with /s or /v.

/n:*xx* formats a disk with *xx* sectors per track. (Available only in MS-DOS versions 3.2 and later and in PC-DOS versions 3.3 and later.)

/t:*yy* formats a disk with *yy* tracks. (Available only in MS-DOS versions 3.2 and 3.3 and PC-DOS version 3.3.)

/f:*size* specifies the size of the floppy disk to format. The following sizes are supported:

Disk type	Size specifier
160 KB	160, 160K, 160KB
180 KB	180, 180K, 180KB
320 KB	320, 320K, 320KB
360 KB	360, 360K, 360KB

(continued)

continued
Disk type   **Size specifier**
720 KB*   720, 720K, 720KB
1.2 MB   1200, 1200K, 1200KB, 1.2, 1.2M, 1.2MB
1.44 MB*   1400, 1400K, 1400KB, 1.44, 1.44M,
                       1.44MB

* 720 KB and 1.44 MB are 3½" disks.

/s creates a system (bootable) disk. If used, this must be the last switch on the command line.

The following table shows the valid switches for various types of disks:

Disk type	Valid switches
160/180 KB	/1 /4 /8 /b /n:*xx* /t:*yy* /v /s /f:*size*
320/360 KB	/1 /4 /8 /b /n:*xx* /t:*yy* /v /s /f:*size*
720 KB*	/n:*xx* /t:*yy* /v /s /f:*size*
1.2 MB	/n:*xx* /t:*yy* /v /s /f:*size*
1.44 MB*	/n:*xx* /t:*yy* /v /s /f:*size*
hard disk	/v /s

* 720 KB and 1.44 MB are 3½" disks.

Warning: If you don't specify a drive, you risk formatting your hard disk or system floppy disk. Before you press the Enter key, be sure that you have specified the correct drive. Also, you should not use the Format command with drives affected by a Join or a Substitute command. You cannot format disks in a drive assigned to a network. The Format command ignores drive reassignments made with an Assign command.

Examples:

To format the floppy disk in drive B and give it a volume label, type:

```
format b: /v
```

Format prompts you for a volume label after the format operation is completed.

To create a system (bootable) floppy disk in drive B, type:

```
format b: /s
```

Graphics

Syntax:

graphics [*printer*] [*profile*] [/b][/c][/f][/lcd][/p=*port*][/r]
   [/printbox:*id*]

Description:

Enables DOS to print graphics on any of several types of printers.

printer is one of the following:

Option	Printer type
color1	IBM Personal Computer Color Printer or compatible with a black ribbon.
color4	IBM Personal Computer Color Printer or compatible with a red-green-blue-black ribbon.
color8	IBM Personal Computer Color Printer or compatible with a cyan-magenta-yellow-black ribbon.
compact	IBM Personal Computer Compact Printer or compatible. (Available only in versions 3.2 and 3.3.)
graphics	IBM Personal Graphics Printer or compatible.
graphicswide	IBM Personal Graphics Printer with 11-inch–wide carriage. (Available only in version 4.)
thermal	IBM PC Convertible Thermal Printer (Available only in versions 4 and later.)

The default is graphics.

profile is the name of the file that contains printer information. If you omit *profile*, the file GRAPHICS.PRO is used. (Available only in version 4.)

/b tells DOS to print the background color as well as the foreground color if you specified *color4* or *color8*. (Not available in PC-DOS versions 2.x.)

/c centers the printout. This switch works only on a
640×200 image (rotated by default) or on a 320×200 image
rotated using the /f switch. (Available only in MS-DOS versions 3.2 and 3.3.)

/f rotates the printout 90 degrees. This switch works only
with a 320×200 image. (Available only in MS-DOS versions
3.2 and 3.3.)

/lcd prints the image from the liquid crystal display (LCD)
screen of the IBM PC Convertible. (Available only in versions 3.3 and later.)

/p=*port* allows the user to specify which port *printer* is attached to. Valid settings are 1 (LPT1), 2 (LPT2), or 3
(LPT3). The default is 1. (Available only in MS-DOS versions 3.2 and 3.3.)

/r tells DOS to print the screen as you see it—light characters on a dark background. (Not available in PC-DOS versions 2.x.)

/printbox:*id* selects the print-box size. *id* should match the
first operand of a Printbox statement in *profile*. (Available
only in version 4.)

After you enter the Graphics command and appropriate parameters, pressing Shift-PrtSc prints everything on the
screen of the active display, including graphics images. On
a noncolor printer, the Graphics command causes the contents of the screen to print in four shades of gray. You
needn't enter the Graphics command again until the next
time you start DOS.

Note: Not all printers can print graphics.

Example:

To print graphics, including the background color, on an
IBM Personal Computer Color Printer with a red-green-
blue-black ribbon, type:

```
graphics color4 /b
```

Graphics Table

Syntax:

graftabl [*nnn* ¦ /status ¦ ?]

Description:

Enables DOS to display special graphics characters (ASCII characters 128 through 255) when the Color/Graphics Adapter is in graphics mode.

nnn is the number of the code page whose character set you want to use:

Number	Code page
437	American (English)
850	Multilingual
860	Portuguese
863	French-Canadian
865	Nordic

/status causes Graftabl to display the active code page. (Can be abbreviated as /sta.)

? causes Graftabl to display the active code page and a list of the switches you can use with Graftabl.

If you omit all parameters, Graftabl loads code page 437.

Versions of Graftabl prior to 3.3 do not support any switches. These versions use only one character set, which is built into Graftabl.

This command is available only in PC-DOS versions 3.0 and later and in MS-DOS versions 3.2 and later.

In versions prior to 3.3, you can load Graftabl only once; to disable it, you must reboot the computer.

Examples:

To load the special graphics table (loading the default code page in versions 3.3 and later), type:

```
graftabl
```

If you want to load the Nordic (Norwegian and Danish) character set or you want to change to the Nordic character set after another character set was previously loaded with a Graftabl command, type:

```
graftabl 865
```

Join

Syntax:

join [*drive1: drive2:path*] [/d]

Description:

Allows the entire directory structure of a drive to be joined, or spliced, into an empty subdirectory of a disk in another drive. After a join, the entire directory structure of the disk in the first drive, starting at the root, together with all files that it contains, appears to be the directory structure of the specified subdirectory on the disk in the second drive; the first drive letter is no longer available.

drive1: is the drive whose entire directory structure will be referenced by *drive2:path*.

drive2:path is the location of the subdirectory to which *drive1:* is to be joined. *path* must be a subdirectory of the root directory of *drive2:*. If *path* already exists, it must be empty; if it doesn't exist, Join creates it.

/d deletes any existing joins that involve *drive1:*. Use this switch only if *drive1:* is the only other parameter in the command line.

If you omit all parameters, Join displays a list of any joins in effect.

The following commands do not work on drives affected by the Join command:

Backup	**Format**
Chkdsk	Label
Diskcomp	Recover

(continued)

continued

Backup	**Format**
Diskcopy	Restore
Fdisk	System

Note: You cannot use the Join command with a drive affected by an Assign or a Substitute command or with a drive assigned to a network.

This command is available only in versions 3.1 and later.

Examples:

If you have an application program that takes up most of a floppy disk and you need a lot of disk space for data files, put the application program disk in drive A and a blank formatted disk in drive B. Then tell DOS to treat the disk in drive B as if it were a directory named \DATA on the disk in drive A by typing:

```
join b: a:\data
```

The join remains in effect until you restart DOS or cancel the join by typing:

```
join b: /d
```

Keyboard

Syntax:

keyb [*xx*[,[*nnn*],[[*drive:*][*pathname*]]][/ID:*yyy*]

Description:

Changes the keyboard layout to match a specific language. (Not available in versions 2.x.)

In PC-DOS versions 3.0 through 3.2 and MS-DOS version 3.2, the Keyboard command supports only the *xx* parameter, which is not optional. In these versions, *xx* must immediately follow the command with no spaces; for example, keyb*xx* can be one of the following:

xx code	Country
uk	United Kingdom
gr	Germany
fr	France
it	Italy
sp	Spain

Note: In MS-DOS version 3.2, Keybdv is also available to change to the Dvorak keyboard.

In versions 3.3 and later, *xx* is the two-letter keyboard code, and *nnn* is the code page for the country whose keyboard layout you want to use. In version 4, you can use /ID:*yyy* to specify the keyboard in use for countries with more than one enhanced keyboard (such as France, Italy, and the United Kingdom). The following parameters are supported:

Keyboard code	Code-page number*	Keyboard ID	Keyboard layout
us	437	103	United States (default)
cf	863	058	Canada (French)
fr	437	189 or 120	France
gr	437	129	Germany
it	437	141 or 142	Italy
sp	437	172	Spain
uk	437	166 or 168	United Kingdom
po	860	163	Portugal
sg	437†	000	Switzerland (German)
sf	437†	150	Switzerland (French)
dk	865	159	Denmark
be	437†	120	Belgium
nl	437	143	Netherlands
no	865	155	Norway
la	437	171	Latin America
sv	437	153	Sweden
su	437	153	Finland

* You can use code-page number 850 to obtain the multilingual character set in place of the country-specific code page.

† Not available in IBM versions prior to 4.

Note: You cannot specify a code page that has not been previously prepared with a Mode: Codepage Prepare command.

drive:pathname is the location of KEYBOARD.SYS, the file containing the keyboard layouts. If you do not include this parameter, Keyb looks for the file in the root directory of the system disk.

In versions prior to 3.3, you can load Keyb only once after starting DOS. In versions 3.3 and later, you can use subsequent Keyb commands to change to other layouts. In all versions, you can change back to the default keyboard layout (United States) at any time by pressing Ctrl-Alt-F1 and then return to the Keyb layout you loaded by pressing Ctrl-Alt-F2.

Examples:

If you have a version prior to 3.3 and want to change your keyboard layout to match the layout of a French keyboard, simply type:

```
keybfr
```

If you have version 3.3 or later and want to change to the Norwegian keyboard layout and tell Keyb that the file KEYBOARD.SYS is located in the \DOS directory in drive C, type:

```
keyb no,865,c:\dos\keyboard.sys
```

Label

Syntax:

label [*drive:*][*label*]

Description:

Assigns, changes, or deletes the volume label of a floppy disk or a hard disk.

drive: is the drive that contains the disk whose volume label
is to be altered. If you omit *drive:*, DOS assumes you want
to work with the disk in the current drive.

label is the volume label (a maximum of 11 characters) to
be assigned to the disk in the drive specified. If you omit
label, DOS prompts you to enter the new label or press Enter for none. If a label already exists and you press Enter,
DOS asks whether you want to delete the current label.

This command is available only in PC-DOS versions 3.0 and
later and in MS-DOS versions 3.1 and later.

Note: You cannot use Label with a drive affected by an
Assign, a Join, or a Substitute command or with a drive assigned to a network.

Example:

To assign the volume label DOSDISK to the floppy disk in
drive B, type:

```
label b:dosdisk
```

This action overwrites any existing label. You do not
receive a prompt for confirmation.

Make Directory

Syntax:

mkdir [*drive:*][*path*]*name*

Description:

Creates a directory. (Can be abbreviated md.)

drive: is the drive that contains the disk on which the directory is to be created. If you omit *drive:*, DOS creates the
directory on the disk in the current drive.

path is the existing directory in which the new directory
will be made. If you omit *path*, DOS creates the new directory in the current directory.

name is the name of the new directory and can be a maximum of eight characters long. You must precede *name* by a backslash if you use *path*.

Note: Because the Assign, Join, and Substitute commands can mask the real identities of directories, you shouldn't create directories when those commands are in effect.

Example:

To create the directory \REPORTS in the existing directory \MKT on the disk in drive B, type:

```
md b:\mkt\reports
```

Memory

Syntax:

mem [/program ¦ /debug]

Description:

Displays the amounts of used and free memory and lists allocated and free memory areas and loaded programs. (Available only in version 4.)

/program displays, in addition to the total memory usage, a list of the programs loaded in memory.

/debug displays, in addition to the total memory usage, a list of the programs loaded in memory, a list of internal drivers, and other programming information.

If you include neither switch, Mem displays only the amounts of used and free memory.

Example:

To display all programs loaded in memory and total memory usage, type:

```
mem /program
```

Mode: Align Display   (CGA)

Syntax:

mode [*display*],*shift*[,t]

Description:

Lets you center the image on a display attached to the Color/Graphics Adapter. Has no effect if you are using an Enhanced Graphics Adapter.

display is one of the values listed under Mode: Select Display. You cannot specify *mono* for the Align Display form of Mode. If you omit *display*, you must still include the comma before *shift*.

shift is either *r* (right) or *l* (left), which causes Mode to shift the image two columns on an 80-column display or one column on a 40-column display.

t causes Mode to display a test pattern. Mode then asks whether the screen display is aligned properly and shifts it in the direction indicated until you respond that it is aligned.

After you use Mode to align the display, Mode clears the screen.

This command is available in all versions of PC-DOS and in MS-DOS versions 3.2 and later.

Example:

To display 80 columns in color, shift the display two columns to the right, and generate a test pattern, type:

```
mode co80,r,t
```

Then respond to the prompt until the display is properly centered.

Mode: Codepage Prepare

Syntax:

mode *device* codepage prepare=((*nnn*) [*drive:*][*path*]*filename*)

Description:

Prepares one or more code pages for use by a specified device. (Available only in versions 3.3 and later.)

device is the name of the device for which the code page is being prepared. Valid device names are CON, PRN, LPT1, LPT2, and LPT3.

nnn is the number(s) of the code page(s) to be used with *device*. You must enclose the number(s) within parentheses. You must then enclose the code-page number(s), their parentheses, and *filename* with another set of parentheses. If you specify more than one code-page number, you must separate the numbers with a space. The following code-page numbers are valid:

Code-page number	Code page
437	American (English)
850	Multilingual
860	Portuguese
863	French-Canadian
865	Nordic

drive:path is the location of *filename*. If you omit *drive:path*, Mode looks for *filename* in the root directory of the disk used to boot the system.

filename is the code-page information (.CPI) file that contains font information for *device*. This parameter is not optional. The following code-page information files are included in PC-DOS versions 3.3 and later; MS-DOS versions 3.3 and later can contain other files:

EGA.CPI	Enhanced Graphics Adapter (EGA) or IBM PS/2 video adapter
4201.CPI	IBM 4201 Proprinter family and Proprinter XL
4208.CPI	IBM Proprinter X24 and XL24
5202.CPI	IBM Quietwriter III printer
LCD.CPI	IBM PC Convertible liquid crystal display (LCD)

You can abbreviate codepage as cp and prepare as prep.

Example:

To prepare code pages 437 and 850 for an Enhanced Graphics Display adapter, specifying C:\DOS\EGA.CPI as the code-page information file, type:

```
mode con cp prep=((437 850) c:\dos\ega.cpi)
```

Mode: Codepage Refresh

Syntax:

mode *device* codepage refresh

Description:

Restores a previously selected code page that was erased from memory for a particular device. (Available only in versions 3.3 and later.)

device is the name of the device (CON, PRN, LPT1, LPT2, or LPT3) whose most recently selected code page is being restored.

You can abbreviate codepage as cp and refresh as ref.

Example:

To restore the most recently selected code page for the printer attached to the second parallel printer port, type:

```
mode lpt2 cp ref
```

Mode: Codepage Select

Syntax:

mode *device* codepage select=*nnn*

Description:

Selects a code page for a particular device. (Available only in versions 3.3 and later.)

device is the name of the device for which the code page is being selected. Valid device names are CON, PRN, LPT1, LPT2, and LPT3.

nnn is the number of the code page to be used with *device*. The following code-page numbers are valid:

Code-page number	Code-page
437	American (English)
850	Multilingual
860	Portuguese
863	French-Canadian
865	Nordic

The code page specified by *nnn* must have been previously prepared with the Mode: Codepage Prepare command.

You can abbreviate codepage as cp and select as sel.

Example:

To select code page 850 for the console, type:

```
mode con cp sel=850
```

Mode: Codepage Status

Syntax:

mode *device* codepage [/status]

Description:

Displays the code-page status of a particular device. (Available only in versions 3.3 and later.)

device is the name of the device whose code-page status is to be displayed. Valid device names are CON, PRN, LPT1, LPT2, and LPT3.

/status adds no functionality; its presence simply parallels the /status switch for the Mode: Device Status command. (Available only in version 4.)

You can abbreviate codepage as cp and status as sta.

Example:

To display the code-page status of the first parallel printer port, type:

```
mode lpt1 cp
```

Mode: Configure Keyboard

Syntax:

mode con[:] rate=*xx* delay=*y*

Description:

Controls the rate at which a key repeats and how soon it begins repeating when held down.

xx is the typematic interval time (1–32).

y is a number from 1 through 4 that corresponds to an auto-repeat start-delay time of ¼, ½, ¾, and 1 second, respectively.

Example:

To set the typematic interval to 12 and the auto-repeat start-delay time to ½ second, type:

```
mode con rate=12 delay=2
```

Mode: Configure Printer

Syntax:

mode LPT*n*[:][*xxx*][,[*y*][,p]]

or

mode LPT*n*[:][*xxx*][,[*y*][,*action*]

or

mode LPT*n*[cols=*xxx*][lines=*y*][retry=*action*]

Description:

Controls the line width and spacing of a printer attached to a parallel port.

LPT*n* is the name of the parallel printer port (LPT1, LPT2, or LPT3). You must specify a printer port.

xxx is the number of characters to print per line (80 or 132). The default is 80. If you omit *xxx* or if you omit cols=*xxx* in version 4, Mode leaves the current width unchanged.

y is the number of lines per inch (6 or 8). The default is 6. If you omit *y* or if you omit lines=*y* in version 4, Mode leaves the current spacing unchanged.

p causes DOS to continually retry to send output if the printer is not ready. (Available only in versions 3.3 and earlier.)

action is the retry action DOS takes if the printer is busy. (Available only in version 4.)

The following values are supported:

Action code	Retry action
e	Return error
b	Return busy
r	Return ready
none	No retry action

Note: retry=b is equivalent to the p parameter in versions 3.3 and earlier.

p, *action*, and retry=*action* cause part of Mode to remain resident in memory. To stop the retry loop, you can press Ctrl-Break.

If you omit an optional parameter (except p or *action*) from the first two forms of the command, you must still type the comma that precedes it; DOS assumes the default setting for the omitted parameter. (*xxx* without any other parameters requires no commas.)

The first form of this command shown on the preceding page is available in all versions of PC-DOS through 3.3 and in MS-DOS versions 3.2 and 3.3; the second and third forms of this command are available only in version 4.

Example:

In version 4, to set the spacing of LPT2 to 132 characters per line, leave the line spacing unchanged, and specify continuous retries, type:

```
mode lpt2:132,,b
```

or

```
mode lpt2 cols=132 retry=b
```

Mode: Configure Serial Port

Syntax:

mode COM*m*[:]*bb*[,*x*[,*y*[,*z*[,p]]]]

or

mode COM*m*[:]*bb*[,*x*[,*y*[,*z*[,*action*]]]]

or

mode COM*m* baud=*bb*[parity=*x*][data=*y*][stop=*z*][retry=*action*]

Description:

Controls the parameters of a serial communications port that define the speed and form of the data transmitted.

COM*m* is the name of the communications port (COM1 or COM2; also COM3 and COM4 in version 4).

bb is the number of bits per second to be sent or received (110, 150, 300, 600, 1200, 2400, 4800, or 9600; also 19200 in versions 3.3 and later). You can abbreviate the parameter to the first two digits (for example, 12=1200). You must specify a value for *bb*.

x is the type of error-checking technique to be used. The default is e.

x code	Type of parity
n	none
o	odd
e	even
m*	mark
s*	space

*Available only in version 4

y is the number of data bits (7 or 8; also 5 or 6 in version 4). The default is 7.

z is the number of stop bits (1 or 2; also 1.5 in version 4). The default is 2 if *bb* is 110; otherwise, the default is 1.

p causes DOS to continually retry to send output if the device connected to COM*m* is not ready. (Available only in versions 3.3 and earlier.)

action is the retry action DOS takes if the device connected to COM*m* is busy. (Available only in version 4.) The following values are supported:

Action code	Retry action
e	Return error (default)
b	Return busy
r	Return ready
none	No retry action

retry=b is equivalent to the p parameter in versions 3.3 and earlier.

p, *action*, and retry=*action* cause part of Mode to remain resident in memory. To stop the retry loop, you can press Ctrl-Break.

If you omit an optional parameter (except p or *action*) from the first two forms of the command, you must still type the comma that precedes it; DOS assumes the default setting for the omitted parameter. (*bb* without any other parameters requires no commas.)

The first form of this command shown at the beginning of this entry is available in all versions of PC-DOS through 3.3 and in MS-DOS versions 3.2 and 3.3; the second and third forms of this command are available only in version 4.

Example:

To set the baud rate for COM2 to 300, parity to odd, leave data bits at 7, and set stop bits to 2, type:

```
mode com2:300,o,,2
```

or

```
mode com2 baud=300 parity=o stop=2
```

Mode: Device Status

Syntax:

mode [*device*] [/status]

Description:

Displays the status of devices installed in your system. (Available only in version 4.)

device is the name of the device whose status is to be displayed. Valid device names are CON, LPT1, LPT2, and LPT3. If you omit *device*, Mode displays the status of all devices.

/status is required only when you request the status of a redirected parallel printer. You can abbreviate status as sta.

Example:

To display the status of the second parallel printer port, type:

```
mode lpt2 /sta
```

Mode: Redirect Parallel Printer Output

Syntax:

mode LPT*n*[:][=COM*m*[:]]

Description:

Redirects to a printer attached to a serial port the output that would normally go to a parallel port.

LPT*n* is the name of the parallel printer port whose output is to be redirected (LPT1, LPT2, or LPT3). If you want to cancel any redirection you applied to that port with a previous Mode: Redirect Parallel Printer Output command, enter LPT*n* alone.

COM*m* is the name of the serial communications port (COM1 or COM2; also COM3 and COM4 in version 4) to which output is to be redirected.

Note: Before you can use this form of Mode, you must use a Mode: Configure Serial Port command.

This command is available in all versions of PC-DOS and in MS-DOS versions 3.2 and later.

Examples:

To redirect printer output from LPT2 to COM2, type:

```
mode lpt2=com2
```

To cancel the redirection and restore the printer output to LPT2, type:

```
mode lpt2
```

Mode: Select Display

Syntax:

mode *display*[,*yy*]

or

mode con[:][cols=*xx*][lines=*yy*]

Description:

Selects the active display and controls the number of lines,
the number of characters per line, and whether or not color
is used on a display attached to a color adapter.

display is one of the following values:

mono	Monochrome adapter, 80 columns
40	Color adapter, 40 columns, color unchanged
80	Color adapter, 80 columns, color unchanged
bw40	Color adapter, 40 columns, color disabled
bw80	Color adapter, 80 columns, color disabled
co40	Color adapter, 40 columns, color enabled
co80	Color adapter, 80 columns, color enabled

xx is the number of characters per line (40 or 80). (Available
only in version 4.)

yy is the number of lines on the display (25, 43, or 50). Not
all adapters support all sizes. (Available only in version 4.)

This form of the Mode command clears the screen.

The first form of this command shown above is available in
all versions of PC-DOS and in MS-DOS versions 3.2 and
later; the second form of this command is available only in
version 4.

Example:

To display 40 columns and enable color on a color display
attached to a color adapter, type:

```
mode co40
```

More

Syntax:

more

Description:

Reads lines of text from standard input (by default, the keyboard), passes 23 lines (in versions 3.3 and earlier) or 24 lines (in version 4) to standard output (by default, the video display), displays a line that says -- *More* --, and waits for a key to be pressed before passing the next set of lines; used to review long files or output from commands one screenful at a time.

Because the input and output of the More command can be redirected, input can also come from a file, a device other than the keyboard, or the output from another command. Likewise, you can redirect the output of the More command to a file or to a device other than the video display.

Example:

To display the file REPORT.TXT one screenful at a time, type:

```
type report.txt : more
```

National Language Support Function

Syntax:

nlsfunc [[*drive:*][*path*]*filename*]

Description:

Tells DOS the name and location of the file that contains extended country-specific information, such as date and

time formats and currency symbols. You must use the
Nlsfunc command before you can use the Change Code
Page (Chcp) command.

drive:path is the location of the file containing the country-
specific information. If you omit both of these, Nlsfunc
looks in the root directory of the current drive.

filename is the name of the country-specific information
file, which in most versions of MS-DOS is COUNTRY.SYS.
If you omit *filename*, Nlsfunc assumes that the file is the
one specified in the Country configuration command in
CONFIG.SYS; if there is no Country configuration command in CONFIG.SYS, Nlsfunc assumes that the file is
named COUNTRY.SYS and is located in the root directory
of the current drive.

Example:
To specify C:\DOS\COUNTRY.SYS as the country information file, type:

```
nlsfunc c:\dos\country.sys
```

Path

Syntax:
path [[*drive:*][*path*][;[*drive:*][*path*] . . .]]

Description:
Tells DOS where to look for a command file (a file with a
.EXE, .COM, or .BAT extension).

drive: is the drive to be searched. If you omit *drive:*, DOS
assumes the current drive.

path is the name of the directory or subdirectory to be
searched. If you include *drive:* but omit *path*, DOS assumes
the current directory of *drive:*.

You can enter more than one *drive:*, *path*, or *drive:path* combination by separating them with semicolons.

A Path command followed by only a semicolon removes any search paths previously set with Path.

A Path command with no parameters displays the current search path for command files.

Example:

To set the search path for command files to include the \DOS and \WORD directories in drive C and the \REPORTS directory in drive A, type:

```
path c:\dos;c:\word;a:\reports
```

Print

Syntax:

print [/d:*device*][/b:*bufsize*][/u:*busytick*][/m:*maxtick*]
   [/s:*timeslice*][/q:*size*][/t] [[*drive:*]*pathname*[/c][/p]]
   [[[*drive:*]*pathname*[/c] [/p]] . . .]

Description:

Prints files while the system is doing something else and lets you maintain a list, called the print queue, that holds the names of a maximum of 32 files to be printed.

/d:*device* tells Print which printer to use. If you omit /d:*device*, Print prompts you to make an entry. The default is PRN. (Not available in versions 2.x.)

/b:*bufsize* sets the size, in bytes, of the internal buffer. This determines the amount of data Print can read from a file at one time. The range is 512 through 16384, and the default is 512. (Not available in versions 2.x.)

/u:*busytick* is the number of timer ticks that Print waits for a busy printer before giving up its time slice. The range is 1 through 255, and the default is 1. (Not available in versions 2.x and MS-DOS version 3.2.)

/m:*maxtick* is the number of timer ticks for which Print keeps control during each of its time slices. The range is 1 through 255, and the default is 2. (Not available in versions 2.x and MS-DOS version 3.2.)

/s:*timeslice* sets the number of time slices per second during which Print is given control of the system. The range is 1 through 255, and the default is 8. (Not available in versions 2.x and MS-DOS version 3.2.)

/q:*size* tells Print the number of files the print queue can hold. The range is 1 through 32, and the default is 10. (Not available in versions 2.x.)

/t stops all printing. If a document is being printed, printing stops, the paper is advanced to the top of the next page, and all files are removed from the print queue.

drive:pathname is the location and name of the file to be added to or deleted from the print queue. You can specify a list of files by separating the names with spaces. Wildcard characters are permitted.

/c removes the preceding *pathname* and all subsequent *pathname*s (until a /p is encountered) from the print queue. If the document is being printed, printing stops and the paper is advanced to the top of the next page.

/p adds the preceding *pathname* and all subsequent *pathname*s (until a /c is encountered) to the print queue. Print assumes this parameter if you specify only *pathname* in the command line.

Note: In versions 2.x, *drive:pathname* must precede the switches; in all other versions the switches (except /c and /p) must come first.

If you enter the Print command with no parameters, Print displays the list of files in the print queue.

The /b:*bufsize*, /d:*device*, /q:*size*, /m:*maxtick*, /s:*timeslice*, and /u:*busytick* switches configure Print and should be used only the first time Print is entered.

Note: Print stops printing a file after encountering a Ctrl-Z character. Therefore, any file containing a Ctrl-Z character might not print in its entirety. To print such a file, use Copy: Copy a File to a Device and include the /b switch.

Note: You cannot use the Print command with a drive affected by an Assign command.

Examples:

To print the file REPORT.TXT, be sure your printer is turned on and type:

```
print report.txt
```

If you decide you don't want to print REPORT.TXT but would like to print JUNE.RPT, type:

```
print report.txt /c june.rpt /p
```

Prompt

Syntax:

prompt *string*

Description:

Changes the system prompt to *string*.

string is the prompt that is to replace the system prompt.

You may enter any character string you want, or you may enter one of the following $x combinations to produce certain characters or useful information:

$x code	Resulting display
$$	The $ character
$t	The time
$d	The date
$p	The current drive and directory
$v	The DOS version number
$n	The current drive
$g	The > character
$l	The < character
$b	The ¦ character
$q	The = character
$h	A backspace; the previous character is erased
$e	The Escape character
$_	The beginning of a new line on the screen

Note: Any spaces you enter between strings or between $x combinations are displayed on the screen.

Prompt without *string* restores the default system prompt.

This command is not available in PC-DOS version 2.0.

Examples:

To define the system prompt as two lines that show the date and the current drive and directory followed by a greater-than sign, type:

```
prompt $d$_$p$g
```

To restore the system prompt to its standard form, simply type:

```
prompt
```

Recover Files

Syntax:

recover [*drive:*]*pathname*

or

recover *drive:*

Description:

Reconstructs a file from a disk that has bad sectors or re-constructs all files from a disk that has a damaged directory structure.

drive:pathname is the name and location of the file that contains unreadable sectors to be reconstructed. Wildcard characters are not permitted. If you omit *drive:*, Recover assumes the current drive. To reconstruct an entire disk that has a bad directory structure, specify *drive:* without *pathname*.

The Recover command names all recovered files in the form FILE*nnnn*.REC, beginning with FILE0001.REC. When

reconstructing an entire disk, Recover does not restore subdirectories, although it does reconstruct any files contained
in existing subdirectories on the disk with the damaged
directory.

Note: Do not use Recover with a drive affected by a Join
or a Substitute command. You cannot use Recover with a
drive assigned to a network.

Examples:

To reconstruct the file REPORT.TXT from the disk in drive
B that has bad sectors, type:

```
recover b:report.txt
```

To reconstruct all files from the disk in drive B that has a
bad directory structure, type:

```
recover b:
```

Remove Directory

Syntax:

rmdir [*drive:*]*path*

Description:

Removes (deletes) a directory. (Can be abbreviated rd.)

drive: is the drive that contains the disk with the directory
to be removed. If you omit *drive:*, Rmdir assumes that the
directory is on the disk in the current drive.

path is the name of the directory to be removed. The directory must not contain files or have any subdirectories. You
must specify *path* because Rmdir cannot remove the current
directory.

Example:

To remove the \LETTERS directory from a directory called
\ENG, type:

```
rd \eng\letters
```

Rename

Syntax:

rename [*drive:*]*pathname filename*

Description:

Changes the name of a file. (Can be abbreviated ren.)

drive:pathname is the current name and location of the file to be renamed.

filename is the new name to be given to the file. Wildcard characters are permitted in both names. You cannot precede *filename* with a drive name or a path; the newly named file is left in the same directory of the same drive.

If *pathname* doesn't exist or another file with the same name as *filename* already exists in that directory, Rename displays an error message and returns to the command level.

Examples:

To change the name of the file ANNUAL.BGT on the disk in the current drive to FINAL.BGT, type:

```
rename annual.bgt final.bgt
```

To change the extension of each file in the current drive and directory from .DOC to .TXT, type:

```
rename *.doc *.txt
```

Replace

Syntax:

replace [*drive1:*]*pathname* [*drive2:*][*path*]
    [/a][/d][/u][/p][/r][/s][/w]

Description:

Selectively adds or replaces files on a disk so that you can update the destination disk with more recent versions of files from the source disk.

drive1:pathname specifies the source of the new file(s). Wildcard characters are permitted.

drive2:path specifies the destination location of the file(s).

/a transfers only source files that do not already exist at the destination. Cannot be used with /s, /d, or /u.

/d or /u replaces only source files with a more recent date than their destination counterparts have. Cannot be used with /a. (/d is available only in MS-DOS version 3.2; /u is available only in version 4.)

/p prompts for confirmation before each file is transferred.

/r specifies that destination files marked read-only can be overwritten.

/s searches all subdirectories of the destination directory for a match with the source files. Cannot be used with /a.

/w causes Replace to wait for the user to press any key before transferring files, thereby allowing the user to change disks.

This command is available only in versions 3.2 and later.

Examples:

To replace all files on the disk in drive B with any newer versions of the same files from the \PROGRAMS directory on the disk in drive A, type:

```
replace a:\programs\*.* b:
```

To transfer only files from the disk in drive A that do not already exist on the disk in drive B, type:

```
replace a:*.* b: /a
```

Restore

Syntax:

restore *drive1:* [*drive2:*][*pathname*] [/s][/p][/b:*date*][/a:*date*]
   [/e:*time*][/L:*time*][/m][/n]

Description:

Restores files that were backed up with the Backup
command.

drive1: is the drive that contains the backup floppy disk.
You *must* include *drive1:*.

drive2: is the drive to which you are restoring the file or
files. If you omit *drive2:*, the file is restored to the current
drive.

pathname is the directory to which you are restoring the
file and the name of the file, including its extension. Wildcard characters are permitted. If you specify a directory,
you *must* also specify a filename. If you omit *pathname* en-
tirely, DOS restores to *drive2:* all files that were backed up
from the current directory. If you specify only a filename,
DOS restores that file to the current *drive2:* directory. You
must specify either *drive2:* or *pathname*.

/s restores all files in the subdirectories of the specified
directory.

/p prompts for confirmation before restoring hidden files,
read-only files, and files that were changed since they were
last backed up.

/b:*date* restores files modified on or before *date*. The date
format depends on whether the Country command is in
effect; the default is *mm-dd-yy*.

/a:*date* restores files modified on or after *date*.

/e:*time* restores files modified at or before *time*. The time
format depends on whether the Country command is in
effect; the default is *hh:mm:ss*.

/L:*time* restores files modified at or after *time*.

/m restores only files modified since the last backup.

/n restores only files that do not exist on the destination disk.

Versions of PC-DOS prior to 3.3 support only the /s and /p switches.

PC-DOS versions 3.0 and later and MS-DOS versions 3.1 and later support all media combinations.

Note: Versions 3.3 and later do not restore the following system files: IBMBIO.COM and IBMDOS.COM for PC-DOS; IO.SYS and MSDOS.SYS for MS-DOS; and COMMAND.COM for both PC-DOS and MS-DOS. You must first use the System command and then use the Copy command (for COMMAND.COM) to restore these files.

Example:
To restore all the files in drive A that were backed up from the \MKT\WP directory in drive B, type:

```
restore a: b:\mkt\wp\*.*
```

Select
(versions 3.x)

Syntax:
select [[a: ¦ b:] *drive:[path]*] *nnn xx*

Description:
Formats and configures a country-specific and language-specific system disk that includes a CONFIG.SYS file that in turn contains the appropriate Country command and an AUTOEXEC.BAT file that contains the appropriate Keyboard command.

a: or b: is the source drive containing the files needed to make the country-specific and language-specific disk. If you omit this parameter, Select assumes drive A.

drive:path is the location of the disk to be formatted and configured for the specified country and the name of the directory for the command files. If you omit this parameter, Select assumes drive B, and the files are placed in the root directory.

nnn is the country code that determines the date and time format after the system is booted with the new disk.

xx is the keyboard code that determines the layout of the keyboard after the system is booted with the new disk.

All country codes and keyboard codes are listed in the following table:

Country	Country code	Keyboard code
Australia	061	US
Belgium	032	BE
Canada (English)	001	US
Canada (French)	002	CF
Denmark	045	DK
Finland	358	SU
France*	033	FR
Germany*	049	GR
International (English)	061	—
Israel	972	—
Italy*	039	IT
Latin America	003	LA
Middle East (Arabic)	785	—
Netherlands	031	NL
Norway	047	NO
Portugal	351	PO
Spain*	034	SP
Sweden	046	SV
Switzerland (French)	041	SF
Switzerland (German)	041	SG
United Kingdom*	044	UK
United States*	001	US

* These are the only choices available in PC-DOS versions 3.0 and 3.1

In versions prior to 3.2, you can specify only *nnn* and *xx* in the command line.

In versions 3.2 and later, if *drive:* is a hard disk, you are prompted to enter the current volume label of the hard disk. If the volume label you enter does not match the existing volume label of the hard disk, Select terminates.

This command is available in PC-DOS versions 3.0 and later and in MS-DOS versions 3.3 and later.

Examples:

To create a system disk configured for use in West Germany using a version of PC-DOS prior to 3.2, place a copy of the original distribution disk in drive A and a blank disk in drive B and then type:

```
select 049 gr
```

(If you have a single-drive system, Select prompts you to change disks.)

To create a system disk configured for use in West Germany using PC-DOS version 3.2, place a copy of the original distribution disk in drive A and a blank disk in drive B and then type:

```
select a: b: 049 gr
```

Select   (version 4)

Syntax:

select menu

Description:

Installs all system files and creates country-specific and language-specific CONFIG.SYS and AUTOEXEC.BAT files. This command is available only in version 4.

menu causes Select to run as a full-screen utility. You must first insert the Install disk in drive A. The menu screens prompt you for all information needed to reconfigure an existing copy of version 4.

If you want to install version 4 on a blank disk or on a disk
that contains an earlier version, you must insert the Install
disk in drive A and reboot your computer by pressing Ctrl-
Alt-Del. Respond to the program's prompts to install version 4.

Example:

To reconfigure an existing copy of version 4, insert the Install disk in drive A, and then enter:

```
a:
select menu
```

Respond to the prompts on the screen.

Set Environment Variable

Syntax:

set [*string*=[*value*]]

Description:

Defines an environment variable name and its value. (An
environment variable associates a value consisting of filenames, pathnames, or other data with a short, symbolic
name that can be easily referenced by programs.)

string is the name of the environment variable.

value is the string of characters, pathnames, or filenames
that defines the current value of *string*.

If you omit *value*, Set deletes the environment variable
name from the environment. If you omit all parameters, Set
displays all the variables in the environment.

Example:

To inform the Microsoft C Compiler that it can find *include*
files in the \INCLUDE directory in drive B, type:

```
set include=b:\include
```

Share

Syntax:

share [/f:*space*][/L:*locks*]

Description:

Loads into the system's memory a module that supports file sharing and locking in a networking environment. This command is available only in versions 3.0 and later.

/f:*space* specifies memory allocation, in bytes, for holding file-sharing information. (The default is 2048.)

/L:*locks* specifies the number of file region locks. (The default is 20.)

Examples:

To load Share into memory using the default values, simply type:

```
share
```

To adjust the memory to 4096 bytes and the file region locks to 40, type:

```
share /f:4096 /L:40
```

Sort

Syntax:

sort [/r][/+*n*]

Description:

Sorts lines of text read from standard input (by default, the keyboard) and sends them to standard output (by default, the video display).

/r sorts lines in reverse alphabetic order (from Z to A).

/+*n* sorts lines starting with the contents in column *n*. (The default is 1.)

Because the input and output of the Sort command can be redirected, input can also come from a file, a device other than the keyboard, or the output from another command. Likewise, you can redirect the output of the Sort command to a file or to a device other than the video display.

Sort does not distinguish between uppercase and lowercase letters.

Examples:

To sort a file in drive B called PHONE.TXT in ascending order based on the character in column 37, type:

```
sort < b:phone.txt /+37
```

To sort a directory listing in reverse alphabetic order, type:

```
dir : sort /r
```

Substitute

Syntax:

subst [*drive1: drive2:path*]

or

subst *drive1:* /d

Description:

Lets you access a directory by a drive letter. After the substitution, DOS automatically replaces any reference to *drive1:* with *drive2:path*.

drive1: is the letter to be used instead of *drive2:path*.

drive2:path is the drive and path that you want to refer to.

/d cancels any substitution in effect for *drive1:*.

If you enter Subst without any parameters, Subst displays a list of substitutions in effect.

This command is available only in versions 3.1 and later.

The following commands do not work on drives affected by the Subst command:

Assign	Diskcomp	Fdisk	Recover
Backup	Diskcopy	Format	Restore
Chkdsk	Fastopen	Label	System

Examples:

To reference the path \MPLAN\SALES\FORECAST in drive C by the drive letter D, type:

```
subst d: c:\mplan\sales\forecast
```

To cancel the substitution, type:

```
subst d: /d
```

System

Syntax:

sys [*drive1*:[*path*]] *drive2*:

Description:

Transfers the DOS system files from the disk in the default or specified drive to the disk in the specified drive.

drive1:path is the location of the system files to be transferred. If you omit *drive1:path*, Sys assumes the current directory in the current drive. (Available only in PC-DOS version 4.)

drive2: is the drive containing the disk to be copied to. The disk must be formatted but completely empty. (See Format.)

Note: In versions 3.3 and later, the system files need not be contiguous. Therefore, you do not have to format the disk in *drive:* if you want to use the Sys command to copy version 3.3 or later onto a disk containing version 3.2 or earlier. (You cannot use Sys to copy PC-DOS version 3.3 or later system files to a disk containing an older version of MS-DOS, or vice versa.)

After the completion of the Sys operation, you can make the disk bootable by copying the file COMMAND.COM to the new disk.

Note: Do not use Sys with a drive affected by the Join or Substitute command. The Sys command ignores drive reassignments made with the Assign command. You cannot use Sys with a drive assigned to a network.

Example:

To transfer the DOS system files from the current drive to the disk in drive B, type:

```
sys b:
```

Time

Syntax:

time [*hh*:*mm*[:*ss*[.*xx*]]][a ¦ p]]

Description:

Sets the system clock.

hh is the hours, based on a 24-hour clock (0 through 23, where 0 is midnight).

mm is the minutes (0 through 59). If you do not include *mm* and specify only *hh*, DOS sets *mm* to 00.

ss is the seconds (0 through 59). This value is optional.

xx is hundredths of a second (0 through 99). This value is optional. If you include it, you must specify *ss*.

a and p specify A.M. and P.M., respectively. If your country code specifies a 12-hour time display, you can enter times without using 24-hour notation. (Available only in PC-DOS version 4.)

No spaces are allowed between parameters.

If you don't include any parameters, Time displays the current setting of the system clock and prompts you to enter the time. If you do not want to change the time, simply press Enter.

You can change the time format by using the Country command in the CONFIG.SYS file. (See Country.)

Example:

To set the time to 8:15 P.M., type:

```
time 20:15
```

Tree

Syntax:

tree [*drive:*][*path*] [/f][/a]

Description:

Displays the path and, optionally, lists the contents of each directory and subdirectory on a disk.

drive: is the drive whose directory structure is to be displayed. If you omit *drive:*, Tree displays the directory structure of the current drive.

path is the uppermost directory to be shown by Tree. If you omit *path* but include *drive:*, Tree displays the entire directory structure of *drive:*. If you omit *drive:* and *path*, Tree displays the structure of the current drive beginning at the current directory. (Available only in version 4.)

/f displays the name of each file in each directory and subdirectory.

/a causes Tree to use standard ASCII characters instead of graphics characters. (Available only in version 4.)

This command is available in all versions of PC-DOS and in MS-DOS versions 3.2 and later.

Example:

Suppose the disk in drive B contains many files stored in various directories. To find out which files are stored in which directories, type:

```
tree b: /f
```

Type

Syntax:

type [*drive:*]*pathname*

Description:

Displays the contents of a file.

drive:pathname is the name and location of the file to be displayed. Wildcard characters are not permitted. If you omit *drive:*, Type assumes the file is on the disk in the current drive.

If the file you name doesn't exist, Type displays *File not found* and returns to the command level.

Note: If you use the Type command to display an executable file (a file with a .EXE or .COM extension) or a binary file created by an application, you'll probably hear beeps and see unintelligible characters on the screen, including graphics symbols. You cannot view such files with the Type command.

Example:

To display the contents of REPORT.JAN, located in the REPORTS directory in the current drive, type:

```
type \reports\report.jan
```

Verify

Syntax:

verify [on ¦ off]

Description:

Sets an internal switch that controls disk write verification.

If Verify is on, DOS checks to see whether the data was written correctly to disk (no bad sectors).

If you enter no parameters, Verify displays the current status of the verify switch. The default condition is off.

Example:
To turn on the verify switch, type:

```
verify on
```

Version

Syntax:
ver

Description:
Displays the version number of DOS that is being used.

Example:
To determine which version of DOS you are currently running, type:

```
ver
```

Version replies with the full name and number.

Volume

Syntax:
vol [*drive:*]

Description:
Displays the volume label and serial number assigned to the specified disk, if they exist.

drive: is the drive that contains the disk whose volume label and serial number are to be displayed. If you omit *drive:*, Vol displays the volume label and serial number of the disk in the current drive.

Vol displays only the volume label in versions 3.3 and earlier.

Example:

To display the volume label and serial number of the disk in drive B, type:

```
vol b:
```

Xcopy   (Extended Copy)

Syntax:

xcopy [*drive:*]*pathname1* [*drive:*][*pathname2*] [/a][/d:*date*][/e]
[/m][/p][/s][/v][/w]

Description:

Copies files. Optionally copies directories and their sub-directories if they exist.

drive:pathname1 is the name and location of the source file. If you specify only a drive, Xcopy copies all files in the current directory of the specified drive. If you specify only a path without a filename, Xcopy copies all files from the specified path in the current drive. You must specify at least one of the source parameters.

drive:pathname2 is the name and location of the target file. Wildcard characters are permitted in both filenames. If you do not specify a destination, Xcopy assumes the current directory of the current drive.

If you specify a drive other than the current drive for *drive:pathname1* and omit *drive:pathname2*, *pathname1* is copied to the current directory of the current drive. If you specify only a drive for *pathname2*, *pathname1* is copied to the disk in the drive you specify and given the same filename.

/a copies source files that have their archive bit set. It does not modify the archive bit of the source file.

/d:*date* copies source files modified on or after the date specified. The date format depends on whether the Country command is in effect; the default is *mm-dd-yy*.

/e copies subdirectories even if they are empty. You must use the /s switch if you use the /e switch.

/m copies source files that have their archive bit set and then turns off the archive bit in the source file.

/p prompts you to confirm whether you want to create each destination file.

/s copies directories and their subdirectories, unless they are empty. If you omit this switch, Xcopy works within a single directory.

/v verifies each file as it is written to the target to ensure that the target files are identical to the source files.

/w causes Xcopy to wait for you to press a key before it starts the copy process, allowing you to change disks.

This command is available only in versions 3.2 and later.

Example:

To copy all files, directories, and subdirectories (including the empty ones) from drive A to drive B and verify that all files were copied intact, type:

```
xcopy a:*.* b: /e /s /v
```

Batch Commands

A batch file is simply a collection of DOS commands. It is a useful way to execute a series of commands that you use frequently. In addition to the standard DOS commands, your batch file can include a set of special commands that let you write simple programs with decision points and replaceable parameters. (A replaceable parameter, an integer between 0 and 9 preceded by a % symbol, is replaced by arguments you type in the command line when you start the batch file.) One of the most commonly used batch files is the AUTOEXEC.BAT file that DOS reads whenever you start up or reboot your system. This file might let you enter the current date, select the display colors, and load a program, without requiring you to type each command separately. AUTOEXEC.BAT must be located in the root directory of the disk from which you boot DOS.

You can create or modify a batch file with any word processor capable of creating text-only (ASCII) files or with Edlin, the DOS text editor. Simply type in the DOS commands in order of execution and then save the file. All batch files must have the extension .BAT, although the extension need not be typed on the command line when you run the file.

To execute a batch file, simply type its name at the system prompt. DOS then sequentially performs the commands the batch file contains.

The following file, ARCHIVE.BAT, demonstrates the use of batch commands. The program copies files from drive B to the \BAK directory in drive C. It first turns off Echo and clears the screen and then checks to see whether you typed any filenames on the command line. If you didn't, the program displays a message and stops. Otherwise, it prompts

you to put a disk in drive B and press a key when you're
ready to continue; then it sequentially copies the files you
included after the batch-file name.

```
@echo off
cls
rem At the command prompt, type the
rem batch file name followed by the
rem names of the files in drive B
rem that you want stored in the \BAK
rem directory in drive C.
if not "%1"=="" goto start
echo You must follow ARCHIVE with a
echo list of files!
goto end
:start
echo Insert the disk containing the
echo files to archive in drive B.
pause
:loop
for %%f in (b:%1) do copy %%f c:\bak
shift
if not exist b:%1 goto end
goto loop
:end
```

To execute ARCHIVE.BAT and store the files PROG1.C,
PROG2.C, and PROG3.C from the disk in drive B to the
\BAK directory in drive C, type:

```
archive prog1.c prog2.c prog3.c
```

@

Syntax:

@ *command*

Description:

Prevents commands in a batch file from being displayed
when DOS executes them. (Available only in versions 3.3
and later.)

command is any DOS command line. The @ symbol must precede *command*.

A common use of the @ symbol is to hide the first *echo off* statement in a batch file.

Call

Syntax:

call [*drive:*][*path*]*batchfile* [*parameters*]

Description:

Lets you carry out the commands in a second batch file and then return to the original batch file and continue with the next command. Call lets you use a batch command you create exactly as you would use any other DOS command. (Available only in versions 3.3 and later.)

drive:path is the location of *batchfile*. If you omit *drive:* or *path*, DOS assumes the current drive or path. If you omit both, DOS assumes the current drive and directory.

batchfile is the name of the batch file you want DOS to execute.

parameters represents any parameters that *batchfile* requires. Either you can enter the parameters themselves, or you can use replaceable parameters so that parameters sent to the current batch file are passed along to the batch file being called.

Echo

Syntax:

echo [on ¦ off ¦ *message*]

Description:

Controls whether commands in a batch file are displayed as they are carried out. Also lets you display your own messages.

If you specify Echo on (the default), commands are displayed; if you specify Echo off, they are not.

message specifies your own message and is displayed even if you previously turned off Echo.

To display a blank line on the screen in versions 2.x, type a space after the Echo command and press Enter. To display a blank line in version 3.0, type a space after Echo, hold down the Alt key, and press 255 on the numeric keypad; finally, release the Alt key and press Enter. To display a blank line in versions 3.1 and later, type a period after Echo and press Enter.

If you omit all options, DOS tells you whether Echo is on or off.

For

Syntax:

for *%%variable* in (*set*) do *command*

Description:

Allows you to carry out a DOS command on one or more files.

%%variable is the name of a variable that is assigned, in turn, each value in *set*. The name should not be any of the numerals 0 through 9.

set is the list of filenames (or replaceable parameters representing filenames) that are assigned to *%%variable* in sequence. You must separate the filenames or parameters with spaces and enclose the entire list in parentheses. Wildcard characters are permitted.

command is any DOS command other than the For command and can include both replaceable parameters (such as %1) specified in the command line and the For command's own replaceable parameter (*%%variable*). (See ARCHIVE.BAT at the beginning of this section for an example of the use of replaceable parameters.)

Goto

Syntax:

goto *label*

Description:

Tells DOS to go to a specific line in the batch file, rather than to the next command in the sequence, and resume execution.

label is a string that identifies the line in the batch file where DOS is to resume execution. The label referred to must appear on a line by itself and begin with a colon.

If

Syntax:

if [not] *condition command*

Description:

Checks whether a condition is true. If it is, DOS carries out the specified command, unless you include the parameter word not, in which case DOS carries out the command if the condition is not true.

condition is the condition to be evaluated and takes one of
three forms:

errorlevel *number*   True if the previous program executed by
                        COMMAND.COM had an exit code of
                        number or higher.

string1==*string2*   True when *string1* and *string2* are
                        identical. Uppercase or lowercase is
                        significant.

exist *filename*   True if *filename* exists. You can include a
                        drive and path, and wildcard characters
                        are permitted.

command is any DOS command and can include replaceable
parameters (such as %1) representing parameters specified
in the command line. (See ARCHIVE.BAT at the beginning
of this section for an example of the use of replaceable
parameters.)

Pause

Syntax:

pause [*message*]

Description:

Causes DOS to pause, display the line *Strike a key when
ready* (or *Press any key to continue* in version 4), and wait
for you to press any key, giving you time to read a message
or complete such preparations as turning on your printer or
changing disks. Also lets you display your own message.

message is a string of characters containing your own message, such as a reminder or a warning. It is displayed only
if Echo is on.

Remark

Syntax:

rem [*message*]

Description:

Displays a message if Echo is on; lets you include hidden explanatory notes in your batch files if Echo is off.

message is a string of characters containing your message or comments. If you do not want comments displayed on your screen, you must include Echo off at the beginning of your batch file or precede the Rem command with the @ symbol. (@ is available only in versions 3.3 and later.)

Shift

Syntax:

shift

Description:

Discards the contents of the %0 replaceable parameter (the parameter containing the batch-file name) and shifts the contents of each subsequent parameter to a lower number. (%1 becomes %0, %2 becomes %1, and so on.)

Batch files can handle only 10 replaceable parameters (%0 through %9) at a time. By moving an eleventh parameter into %9, Shift lets you specify more than 10 arguments in the command line. You can use Shift as often as necessary to process all arguments. With each shift, the current contents of %0 are lost and cannot be recovered.

Configuration Commands

Unlike other DOS commands, which tell DOS *what* to do, configuration commands tell DOS *how* to do something, such as use a device or communicate with a disk drive. You will need these commands infrequently, usually only when you add a device to your computer system (thereby changing its *configuration*).

Configuration commands are not typed at the keyboard; you put them in a special file called CONFIG.SYS that must be in the root directory of the DOS disk you use to boot the system. DOS carries out these commands only when it is started; therefore, if you change a configuration command in CONFIG.SYS, you must restart DOS for the command to take effect.

Some application programs require you to add certain commands to the CONFIG.SYS file so that the application can run properly; for example, an application might require that DOS be able to work with more files than the eight it is allowed by default.

You can create or modify a CONFIG.SYS file with any word processor that can create text-only (ASCII) files or with Edlin, the DOS text editor. You can add or change any of the configuration commands explained in this section. Each command must be on a separate line, as shown in the following example:

```
break=on
buffers=20
device=c:\dos\ansi.sys
device=mouse.sys
drivparm=/d:1 /s:9 /t:80
fcbs=8,4
files=20
lastdrive=z
shell=c:\dos\command.com
```

Break

Syntax:

break=[on ! off]

Description:

Instructs DOS how often it should check for Ctrl-C (or Ctrl-Break), the key sequence you use to terminate a program or batch file.

By default, DOS checks for Ctrl-C each time it reads from or writes to a character device (screen, printer, or serial port). If Break is on, DOS also checks for Ctrl-C each time a system call is made, such as when a disk is read from or written to.

Buffers

Syntax:

buffers=*number* [,*max*] [/x]

Description:

Defines the number of work areas in memory that DOS uses to store data when reading from and writing to disk.

number is the number of buffers you need. In versions prior to 3.3 and in version 4, *number* can be 1 through 99; in version 3.3, *number* can be 2 through 255.

In versions prior to 3.3, the default for *number* is 2 (3 for the IBM PC/AT). In versions 3.3 and later, the default depends on how your system is configured.

Configuration	Default buffers
Base system	2
Floppy-disk drive > 360 KB	3
128 KB to 255 KB RAM	5

Configuration	Default buffers
256 KB to 511 KB RAM	10
512 KB RAM or more	15

Note: Buffers require memory, so you should avoid specifying a *number* greater than 30.

max is the maximum number of sectors (1 through 8) that can be read or written in one I/O operation. The default is 1. (Available only in version 4.)

/x places the buffers in expanded memory. (Available only in version 4.)

Country

Syntax:

country=*nnn*[,[*codepage*][,[*drive:*]*filename*]]

Description:

Tells DOS to follow local conventions for a given country in such matters as date format, currency symbols, and decimal separators. If you do not specify a country, DOS follows the conventions for the country for which that copy of DOS was manufactured. This command is available only in versions 3.0 and later.

nnn is a three-digit country code number from the following list. You must include all three digits, including any zeros at the beginning.

Country	Country code
Middle East (Arabic)	785
Australia	061
Belgium	032
Canada (French)	002
Denmark	045
Finland	358
France	033

(continued)

continued

Country	Country code
Germany	049
Israel	972
Italy	039
Japan*	081
Korea*	082
Latin America*	003
Netherlands	031
Norway	047
People's Republic of China*	086
Portugal	351
Spain	034
Sweden	046
Switzerland	041
Taiwan*	088
United Kingdom	044
United States	001

* Available only in version 4

codepage is a three-digit number that specifies the code page that DOS is to use. (Available only in versions 3.3 and later.)

Code page	Code-page number
American (English)	437
Multilingual	850
Portuguese	860
Hebrew*	862
French-Canadian	863
Arabic*	864
Nordic	865
Japanese†	932
Korean†	934
Simplified Chinese†	936
Traditional Chinese†	938

* Available only with a country supplement in version 4
† Available only on Asian hardware in version 4

drive:filename is the name and location of the file supplied
with your DOS disks that contains country-specific information. If you omit *drive:*, DOS assumes the file is stored in
the root directory of the disk used to boot the system. If you
omit *filename*, DOS assumes the file is COUNTRY.SYS.
(Available only in versions 3.3 and later.)

Device

Syntax:

device=[*drive:*]*pathname*

Description:

Specifies a device driver program (a file with the extension
.SYS) that tells DOS how to use a particular device, such as
a Microsoft Mouse.

drive: is the drive containing the disk on which the program
exists. If you omit *drive:*, DOS assumes the program is on
the disk used to boot the system.

pathname is the location and name of the program—for
example, \DEVICE\MOUSE.SYS for the Microsoft Mouse
driver located in the \DEVICE directory.

If you have more than one device driver to install, you can
use more than one Device command in CONFIG.SYS.

The following device driver programs are normally included with DOS:

Device driver	Included in version
ANSI.SYS	2.0 and later
DISPLAY.SYS	3.3 and later
DRIVER.SYS	3.2 and later
RAMDRIVE.SYS	3.2 and later (MS-DOS only)
SMARTDRV.SYS	4 (MS-DOS only)
VDISK.SYS	3.0 and later (PC-DOS only)
XMA2EMS.SYS	4 (PC-DOS only)
XMAEM.SYS	4 (PC-DOS only)

Drivparm

Syntax:

drivparm=/d:*dd*[/c][/f:*ff*][/h:*hh*][/i][/n][/s:*ss*][/t:*tt*]

Description:

Alters the system's table of characteristics for a specific
block device, overriding the default DOS characteristics.
(Whenever a device such as a disk drive performs input or
output, DOS refers to an internal table of characteristics for
that device.)

/d:*dd* designates the drive number *dd*. (The valid range is 0
through 255, where 0 = drive A, 1 = drive B, and so on.)

/c indicates that the device requires change-line (doorlock)
support.

/f:*ff* designates one of the following device types. (The
default value is 2.)

Value	Device type
0	5¼-inch 320-KB or 360-KB floppy disk
1	5¼-inch 1.2-MB floppy disk
2	3½-inch 720-KB floppy disk
3	8-inch single-density floppy disk
4	8-inch double-density floppy disk
5	Fixed disk
6	Tape drive
7	3½-inch 1.44-MB floppy disk

/h:*hh* indicates the number of read/write heads. (The valid
range is 1 through 99; the default value is 2.)

/i indicates that the device is an electrically compatible
3½-inch disk drive. (Available only in MS-DOS version 4.)

/n indicates that the device is not removable.

/s:*ss* designates the number of sectors per track. (The valid
range is 1 through 99; the default value is 9.)

/t:*tt* designates the number of tracks per side. (The valid range is 1 through 999.)

You can include multiple Drivparm commands (each modifying the characteristics for a different device) in the same CONFIG.SYS file.

This command is available only in MS-DOS versions 3.2 and later.

Fcbs (File Control Blocks)

Syntax:

fcbs=*x,y*

Description:

Tells DOS the maximum number of files that can be open at the same time using file control blocks (FCBs). (FCBs are data structures that reside in an application's memory space and store information about open files.) Also tells DOS not to close automatically a certain number of files.

x is the maximum number of files that can be open concurrently using FCBs. (The valid range is 1 through 255; the default is 4.)

y is the number of files opened with FCBs, counting from the first file, that are protected against automatic closure. (The valid range is 0 through 255; the default is 0.) When DOS needs to open more files than *x*, it closes the least recently used file to make room for the new file. The first *y* files are not included in the ''close'' list. *y* must always be less than or equal to *x*.

This command is available only in PC-DOS versions 3.1 and later and in MS-DOS versions 3.0 and later.

Files

Syntax:

files=*number*

Description:

Tells DOS how many files can be open at one time.

number is the number of files that can be open. (The valid range is 8 through 255; the default is 8.) A practical suggested value is 20.

Install

Syntax:

install=[*drive:*][*path*]*filename* [*parameters*]

Description:

Loads commands during CONFIG.SYS processing.

drive:path is the location of filename. If you omit *drive:* or *path*, Install assumes the root directory of the disk used to boot the system.

filename is the command to be loaded. You must include the file's extension. *filename* must be one of the following:

FASTOPEN.EXE

KEYB.COM

NLSFUNC.EXE

SHARE.EXE

parameters represents any parameters that *filename* requires.

Lastdrive

Syntax:

lastdrive=*letter*

Description:

Specifies the last drive letter DOS recognizes as valid.

letter is a letter from a through z. If you do not include
Lastdrive in a CONFIG.SYS file, the highest drive letter
DOS recognizes as valid is e.

This command is available only in versions 3.0 and later.

Remark

Syntax:

rem [*comment*]

Description:

Allows you to include explanatory notes in a CONFIG.SYS
file. (Available only in version 4.)

comment is any string of characters.

Shell

Syntax:

shell=[*drive:*]*pathname*

Description:

Defines the name and location of the file that contains the command processor. (The command processor, or shell, is your interface to the operating system. The default shell for DOS is COMMAND.COM.)

drive:pathname is the name and location of the file containing the command processor. Optional or required switches and other parameters for the command processor can follow the filename, although the Shell command itself has no switches or parameters.

DOS loads COMMAND.COM from the root directory of the disk used to boot the system unless the CONFIG.SYS file contains a Shell command. The most common use of the Shell command is to advise DOS that COMMAND.COM is stored in a location other than the root directory.

Stacks

Syntax:

stacks=*number,size*

Description:

Reserves memory within DOS for temporary use during hardware interrupts. The Stacks command is required by some application programs. (Available only in versions 3.2 and later.)

number is the number of stacks to be allocated. (The valid range is 0 through 64; the default is 9.)

size is the size of each stack in bytes. (The valid range is 0 through 512; the default is 128.)

For the IBM PC, IBM PC/XT, and IBM Portable PC, the default for both *number* and *size* is 0 (zero).

Switches

Syntax:

switches=/k

Description:

Specifies the use of conventional keyboard functions when an enhanced keyboard is installed. (Available only in PC-DOS 4.)

/k prevents the system from using extended keyboard functions. You must use this switch with the Switches command.

Edlin Commands

Edlin is a simple text editor that lets you:

- Create and save new text (ASCII) files.

- Update existing files and save both the updated and original versions.

- Edit, delete, insert, copy, move, and display lines.

- Search for, delete, or replace text.

The text created or edited with Edlin is divided into lines of varying length, up to 253 characters per line. You must press Enter at the end of each line. (If a line is longer than your screen display, it appears as two or more lines on the screen.)

Line numbers are displayed by Edlin as you edit but are not present in the saved file.

To start Edlin, type:

edlin [*drive:*]*pathname* [/b]

drive:pathname is the name and location of an existing file or of a new file to be created with Edlin.

/b causes Control-Z characters in the file to be ignored.

Once you start Edlin, you will see the Edlin command prompt (an asterisk). You can then enter commands to do such tasks as listing existing lines, inserting lines, moving a range of lines, and replacing strings of characters. When you enter the commands described in this section, it makes no difference whether you type spaces between the variables and the letter specifying the command.

Append

Syntax:

[*number*]**a**

Description:

Reads the number of lines specified from disk into memory.

number is the number of lines to be read. If *number* is not specified or is too large, Edlin reads in lines until available memory is 75 percent full. Only use this command after using the Write command.

Append has no effect if available memory is already 75 percent full.

Copy

Syntax:

[*range*],*line*[,*number*]**c**

Description:

Copies one or more lines to the position specified.

range is the numbers of the starting and ending lines to be copied, separated by a comma. You must enter the comma within *range* even if you omit one or both of the line numbers. If you omit the starting number, the copied lines start with the current line. If you omit the ending number, the copied lines end with the current line. If you omit both numbers, only the current line is copied.

line is the number of the line before which you want to place the copied lines. The previous contents of *line* and the remainder of the file are pushed ahead and renumbered. The first copied line becomes the current line.

The line numbers in *range* and *line* must not overlap.

number indicates how many times the lines should be copied.

Delete

Syntax:

[*range*]**d**

Description:

Deletes one or more lines.

range is the numbers of the starting and ending lines to be deleted, separated by a comma. If you omit the starting number, you must precede the ending number with a comma. If you omit the starting number, the deletion starts at the current line and continues to the ending line. If you omit the ending number, only the starting line is deleted. If you omit both numbers, the current line is deleted. The lines following the deleted lines are pushed back and renumbered. The line following the last deleted line becomes the current line.

Edit Line

Syntax:

[*line*]

Description:

Displays a line of text so that you can edit it.

line is the number of the line to be edited. Enter a period (.) to edit the current line.

If you do not want to edit the line, press Enter at the beginning of the line to leave it unchanged.

End Edit

Syntax:

e

Description:

Stores the edited file and returns to DOS. If you are editing an existing file, this command changes the extension of the original input file to .BAK, overwriting a file with the same name and a .BAK extension if one exists.

Insert

Syntax:

[*line*]i

Description:

Allows you to insert new lines at the specified position.

line is the number of the line before which you want to insert a line. The previous contents of *line* and the remainder of the file are pushed ahead and renumbered. The line following the last inserted line becomes the current line.

If you are beginning a new Edlin text file or simply want to insert lines before the current line, do not include a line number. To insert lines at the end of a file, specify # for *line*. To stop inserting, press Ctrl-C or Ctrl-Break.

List

Syntax:

[*range*]l

Description:

Displays one or more lines.

range is the numbers of the starting and ending lines to be
displayed, separated by a comma. You must enter the
comma within *range* if you omit the starting number. If
you omit the starting number, the list begins 11 lines before
the current line and continues to the ending line. If you
omit the ending number, the list contains 23 lines (24 in
version 4) beginning with the starting line. If you omit
both numbers, the list contains 23 lines (24 in version 4)
centered around the current line. List has no effect on the
current line number.

In versions prior to 4, List scrolls through the entire range
without stopping. To pause the screen, press Ctrl-S; when
you are ready, press any key to resume scrolling. In version
4, List stops every 24 lines and asks you if you want to
continue.

Move

Syntax:

[*range*],*line* **m**

Description:

Moves one or more lines to the position specified.

range is the numbers of the starting and ending lines to be
moved, separated by a comma. You must enter the comma
within *range* even if you omit one or both of the numbers.
If you omit the starting number, the move starts with the
current line. You can substitute a plus sign (+) followed by
a number for the ending number to indicate that you want
to move the current line plus the specified number of subsequent lines. If you omit the ending number, the end of the
move includes the current line. If you omit both numbers,
only the current line is moved.

line is the line before which you want to place the moved lines. The file is automatically renumbered after the move. The first line moved becomes the current line.

The line numbers in *range* and *line* must not overlap.

Page

Syntax:

[*range*]**p**

Description:

Displays one or more lines.

range is the numbers of the starting and ending lines to be displayed, separated by a comma. If you omit the starting number, you must precede the ending number with a comma. If you omit the starting number, the list begins one line past the current line and continues to the ending line. If you omit the ending number, the list contains 23 lines (24 in PC-DOS version 4) beginning with the starting line. If you omit both numbers, the list contains 23 lines (24 in PC-DOS version 4) beginning one line past the current line.

Page differs from List in that it changes the current line to the last line displayed.

Quit

Syntax:

q

Description:

Cancels an editing session and returns to DOS without storing the revised file.

Edlin prompts you for approval before quitting.

Replace

Syntax:

[*range*][?]**r**[*string1*][^Z*string2*]

Description:

Searches for a string and replaces it with a different string.

range is the numbers of the starting and ending lines to be searched, separated by a comma. You must enter the comma within *range* if you omit the starting number. If you omit the starting number, the search starts at one line past the current line. If you omit the ending number, the search continues to the last line. If you omit both numbers, the search starts at one line past the current line and continues to the last line.

? causes Edlin to prompt for confirmation of each change.

string1 is the string to be replaced.

string2 is the string to be substituted for *string1*. If you omit *string2*, the command deletes *string1*. In this case, you must end the command after *string1* by pressing the Enter key. If you do specify *string2*, you must separate the two strings by pressing F6 or Ctrl-Z.

Example:

To replace the word "document" with the word "report" wherever it occurs in lines 20 through 55, type:

```
20,55rdocument^Zreport
```

Search

Syntax:

[*range*][?]**s***string*

Description:

Searches one or more lines for a specified string of characters.

range is the numbers of the starting and ending lines to be searched, separated by a comma. You must enter the comma within *range* if you omit the starting number. If you omit the starting number, the search starts one line past the current line. If you omit the ending number, the search continues to the last line. If you omit both numbers, the search starts one line past the current line and continues to the last line.

? causes Edlin to prompt for confirmation after each occurrence of *string*; press N to continue the search.

string is the string to be searched for. If you type a space after the s, Search considers the space to be part of *string*. The line containing *string* becomes the current line. If you omit *string*, Edlin uses the last search string entered in a Replace or a Search command.

Transfer

Syntax:

[*line*]t [*drive:*][*path*]*filename*

Description:

Copies (merges) another file into the file you're creating or editing.

line is the number of the line before which you want to place the copied lines. If you omit *line*, Edlin inserts the copy before the current line. The previous contents of *line* and the remainder of the file are pushed ahead and renumbered, and *line* becomes the current line.

drive:filename can include a drive letter, a filename, and an extension. In versions 3.0 and later, you can also include a path.

Write

Syntax:

[*number*]**w**

Description:

Writes the number of lines specified from memory to disk.

number is the number of lines to be written, beginning with line 1. Use this command only when editing a file larger than 75 percent of available memory. If you omit *number*, lines are written until a total of 25 percent of memory remains free.

Write has no effect unless memory is at least 75 percent full.

DOS Shell Commands

The DOS Shell, available only in version 4, is an optional, visually oriented means of working with DOS. The Shell always begins by displaying the Main Group on the Start Programs screen (unless you have removed the /MENU startup option from DOSSHELL.BAT). From this screen you can start a program, go to another group, or exit the Shell and return to the command prompt. The figure below illustrates the group structure of the Shell.

```
                         Start Programs
 Program  Group  Exit
                          Main Group
               To select an item, use the up and down arrows.
         To start a program or display a new group, press Enter.

 Command Prompt
 File System
 Change Colors
 DOS Utilities...
```

```
                         Start Programs
 Program  Group  Exit
                        DOS Utilities...
               To select an item, use the up and down arrows.
         To start a program or display a new group, press Enter.

 Set Date and Time
 Disk Copy
 Disk Compare
 Backup Fixed Disk
 Restore Fixed Disk
 Format
```

```
                          File System
 File   Options   Arrange   Exit
 A  B  C
 C:\

 C:\              AUTOEXEC.BAT   126   01-01-90
  ┌DOS            CONFIG.SYS      26   01-01-90
  ├WORD           LETTER.DOC   3,218   01-13-90
  └EXCEL
```

When you install DOS, you decide whether you want the Shell to appear each time you boot your system. If you choose not to start the Shell automatically, you can start it from the DOS command prompt by entering:

DOSSHELL

If you decide later that you want the Shell to start automatically, add the Dosshell command to the end of your AUTOEXEC.BAT file.

The commands in this section are organized as they appear when you first start the Shell. If applicable, the command-prompt equivalent is included. Note that you will generally find differences in performance and features between a Shell command and its command-prompt equivalent.

Start Programs Screen

Program menu:

Start	Starts a program.
	Command-prompt equivalent: Entering the name of an executable file
Add	Adds a program to the current group.
Change	Modifies the title, command(s), help text, or password for an existing program in the current group.
Delete	Removes a program from the current group.
Copy	Copies a program from the current group to another group.

Group menu:

Add	Adds a group to the Main Group.
Change	Modifies the title, filename, help text, or password for an existing group.
Delete	Deletes a group from the Main Group. Any programs within the group are also deleted.
Reorder	Lets you rearrange the order of titles in the current group.

Exit menu:

Exit Shell	Exits the Shell and returns to the command prompt.
	Command-prompt equivalent: Exit
Resume Start Programs	Resumes display of the Start Programs screen.

Main Group title list:

Command Prompt	Exits the Shell and returns to the command prompt.
File System	Displays the File System screen.
Change Colors	Lets you change the Shell's screen colors.
DOS Utilities	Displays the DOS Utilities group.

DOS Utilities group title list:

Set Date and Time	Changes the date and time displayed at the top of the Start Program and File System screens.
	Command-prompt equivalents: Date, Time
Disk Copy	Copies the entire contents of one floppy disk to another.
	Command-prompt equivalent: Diskcopy
Disk Compare	Compares the contents of one floppy disk with the contents of another and lists any differences between them.
	Command-prompt equivalent: Diskcomp
Backup Fixed Disk	Copies files from a hard disk to one or more floppy disks, replacing the previous contents of the floppy disk(s). Refer to the Backup command in the ''DOS Commands'' section for a list of switches you can use with this command.
	Command-prompt equivalent: Backup
Restore Fixed Disk	Copies files created with a previous Backup Fixed Disk command to a hard disk. Refer to the Restore command in the ''DOS Commands'' section for a list of switches you can use with this command.
	Command-prompt equivalent: Restore

Format

Formats a floppy or hard disk for use with DOS. Refer to the Format command in the ''DOS Commands'' section for a list of switches you can use with this command.

Warning: The Format command permanently erases any information currently residing on the disk.

Command-prompt equivalent: Format

File System Screen

File menu:

Open (start)

Starts the selected program, or starts the program associated with the selected file.

Command-prompt equivalent: Entering the name of an executable file

Print

Prints the selected file on your printer.

Command-prompt equivalent: Print

Associate

Associates one or more file extensions with the selected program. When you select a file and choose the Open (start) command, the Shell starts the associated program. An extension can be associated with only one program at a time. You cannot associate more than 20 file extensions in the Shell.

Move

Copies the selected file to the location you specify, and then removes the file from its original location.

Command-prompt equivalent: Copy, Delete

Copy

Copies the selected file to the location you specify. If you are copying the file to the same drive and directory, you must give the copy a different name.

Command-prompt equivalent: Copy

Delete
: Removes the selected file from the disk. If you check the *Confirm on delete* option of the File Options dialog box, you will be prompted for confirmation before the file is deleted.

  Command-prompt equivalent: Delete

Rename
: Renames the selected file(s).

  Command-prompt equivalent: Rename

Change attribute
: Changes the hidden, read-only, or archive attribute of the selected file or files.

  Command-prompt equivalent: Attrib

  Note: You cannot change a file's hidden attribute with the Attrib command.

View
: Displays the contents of the selected file. You can toggle between ASCII and hexadecimal display by pressing F9.

  Command-prompt equivalent: Type

  Note: The Type command displays files in ASCII format only.

Create directory
: Creates a subdirectory in the selected drive and directory.

  Command-prompt equivalent: Mkdir

Select all
: Selects all files in the current directory.

Deselect all
: Deselects all files in the current directory.

Options menu:

Display options
: Lets you selectively display files based on the name and/or extension and determine whether the files will be sorted by name (default), extension, date, size, or the order in which they appear on the disk.

  Command-prompt equivalents: Dir, Sort

File options
: Lets you specify whether or not the Shell will prompt you for confirmation before deleting or replacing a file or directory; also lets you decide whether you want files residing in separate directories to be simultaneously selected.

Show information   Displays information about the currently selected file or files, including name and extension, attributes, size, and location; also displays information about the current drive.

Command-prompt equivalents: Dir, Chkdsk

Arrange menu:

Single file list   Displays only the files that are in the current directory.

Command-prompt equivalent: Dir

Multiple file list   Displays the files that are in two different directories.

System file list   Displays all files in all directories of the current disk drive and information about the selected file.

Exit menu:

Exit File System   Exits the File System screen and returns to the Start Programs screen.

Resume File System   Resumes display of the File System screen.

Keyboard Commands

Key	Action
↑, ←, ↓, →	Moves the selection highlight between options on the screen.
Enter	Carries out the highlighted or selected command.
Esc	Exits a menu or cancels a command before you carry it out.
F1	Displays help for the currently selected item.
Alt-F1	Displays an index of all Help topics while you are in Help.

Key	Action
F2	Saves the information you've typed into a dialog box, or completes a copy operation.
F3	From the File System screen, returns to the Start Programs screen; from the Start Programs screen, exits the Shell and returns to the DOS command prompt; or cancels a copy operation.
F4	Creates the ‖ character that you use to separate commands in a dialog box.
F9	Displays the key assignments while you are in Help or, during the View command, toggles the display between hexadecimal and ASCII.
Shift-F9	Switches to the DOS command prompt.
F10	Moves the selection bar between the menu bar and the selection area of the screen.
F11	Displays an index of all Help topics while you are in Help.
PgUp and PgDn	Scrolls the text while you are in Help, the file displayed by a View command, or a list of files in the File System screen.
Spacebar	Selects or deselects a file in the File System screen.
Tab	Moves between areas in the File System screen and within dialog boxes.
Shift-Tab	Moves between areas in the File System screen and within dialog boxes. The selection moves in the opposite direction from Tab.

Setup Options

If you installed the DOS Shell when you installed version 4 of DOS on your computer, DOS created a file, called DOSSHELL.BAT, that it uses to configure the Shell each time you start it. You can use the following options to modify this file so that it fits your needs.

Warning: Be sure to make a backup copy of your existing DOSSHELL.BAT file before you attempt any modification.

Option	Description
/CLR:SHELL.CLR	Causes DOS to look in the file SHELL.CLR to set up the Shell colors for your display adapter.
/CO1	Causes the Shell to appear in 16-color, high-resolution 640 × 350 graphics mode. You must have the appropriate hardware to use this option. You cannot use this option with /CO2, /CO3, or /TEXT.
/CO2	Causes the Shell to appear in two-color, high-resolution 640 × 480 graphics mode. You must have the appropriate VGA or HGA hardware to use this option. You cannot use this option with /CO1, /CO3, or /TEXT.
/CO3	Causes the Shell to appear in 16-color, high-resolution 640 × 480 graphics mode. You must have the appropriate VGA hardware to use this option. You cannot use this option with /CO1, /CO2, or /TEXT.
/COLOR	Allows you to choose the Change Colors command from the Main Group.
/DATE	Causes the current date and time to be displayed at the top of the Start Programs and File System screens.
/DOS	Lets you access the File System screen to work with files and directories.
/EXIT	Allows you to exit the DOS Shell permanently. If you omit this option, you will not be able to exit the Shell and return to the command prompt.
/LF	Allows left-handed use of the mouse by using the right mouse button instead of the left mouse button.

Option	Description
/MAINT	Lets you add, modify, or remove programs and groups on the Start Programs screen.
/MENU	Activates the Start Programs screen. If you omit this option, the Shell will start at the File System screen.
/MEU:SHELL.MEU	Causes DOS to look in the file SHELL.MEU for the list of programs and groups that will be displayed in the Main Group when you start the Shell.
/MOS:PCIBMDRV.MOS	Allows the Shell to use an IBM mouse.
/MOS:PCMSDRV.MOS	Allows the Shell to use a Microsoft serial mouse. (Available only in PC-DOS.)
/MOS:PCMSPDRV.MOS	Allows the Shell to use a Microsoft parallel mouse. (Available only in PC-DOS.)
/MUL	Causes DOS to keep directory information in memory, increasing performance of the system. If you omit this option, DOS must read information from the disk each time you access a new directory.
/PROMPT	Lets you exit the Shell and return to the DOS command prompt. If you omit this option, you will not be able to exit the Shell.
/SND	Causes the Shell to emit a tone if you make an error while in the Shell.
/SWAP	Allows DOS to save File System directory and file information on a floppy disk when you switch to the Shell command prompt or activate a program.
/TEXT	Causes the Shell to appear in text mode. You cannot use this option with /CO1, /CO2, or /CO3.

Option	Description
/TRAN	Clears the Shell from memory when you exit the Shell. If you omit this option, the Shell will remain in memory when you return to the DOS command prompt.

DOS Editing Keys

Each time you enter a DOS command at the system prompt or enter an Edlin command within Edlin, DOS saves a copy of that command in a special storage area called the template. By using the DOS editing keys, you can duplicate or edit the command in the template; pressing Enter then executes the edited command, saving you the trouble of retyping the command.

Key	Editing function
F1	Copies one character from the template to the command line. You can press F1 repeatedly to copy more than one character. (The right direction key performs the same function.)
F2 *char*	Copies characters up to, but not including, *char* from the template and places them on the command line. If *char* is not in the template, DOS takes no action.
F3	Copies all remaining characters in the template to the command line. You can press F3 and then press Enter to repeat the last DOS or Edlin command quickly.
F4 *char*	Skips over characters in the template up to, but not including, *char*. If *char* is not in the template, DOS takes no action.
F5	Causes the current command line to be placed in the template, replacing the previous command line.
F6	Places a ^Z (Control-Z) character in the command line.
Ins	Toggles between insert mode and overtype mode. The default is overtype mode.
Del	Skips over a character in the template without copying it to the command line.
Esc	Cancels the current operation, leaving the template unchanged.

Note: In Edlin, you can also use the editing keys to edit the contents of an existing line of a file.

Index

Special Character

A

B

C

D

M

N,P

Q,R

S

Van Wolverton

A professional writer since 1963, Van Wolverton has had bylines as a newspaper reporter, editorial writer, political columnist, and technical writer. He wrote his first computer program—one that tabulated political polls—for the *Idaho State Journal* in Pocatello, Idaho, in 1965. His interests in computers and writing have been intertwined ever since. As a computer professional, Wolverton has worked at IBM and Intel and has written software documentation for the major national software companies, including Microsoft Corporation. He is the author of the bestselling *Running MS-DOS* and *Supercharging MS-DOS* and a contributor to *The MS-DOS Encyclopedia*. Wolverton and his wife, Jeanne, live in a twenty-first-century log cabin near Alberton, Montana.

The manuscript for this book was prepared and submitted to Microsoft Press in electronic form. Text files were processed and formatted using Microsoft Word.

Cover design by Celeste Design
Interior text design by Darcie S. Furlan
Principal typography by Carolyn Magruder
Color separations by Rainier Color

Text composition by Microsoft Press in Times Roman with display in Futura Heavy, using the Magna composition system and the Linotronic 300 laser imagesetter.

Printed on recycled paper stock.